T0130020

OUT OF THE FOG

Adventures through Lifestyle Change

ALANA HENDERSON

BALBOA.
PRESS

A DIVISION OF HAY HOUSE

Balboa Press books may be ordered through booksellers or by contacting:

Balboa Press
A Division of Hay House
1663 Liberty Drive
Bloomington, IN 47403
www.balboapress.com.au
1 (877) 407-4847

Because of the dynamic nature of the Internet, any web addresses or links contained in
this book may have changed since publication and may no longer be valid. The views
expressed in this work are solely those of the author and do not necessarily reflect the
views of the publisher, and the publisher hereby disclaims any responsibility for them.

The author of this book does not dispense medical advice or prescribe the use
of any technique as a form of treatment for physical, emotional, or medical
problems without the advice of a physician, either directly or indirectly. The
intent of the author is only to offer information of a general nature to help you
in your quest for emotional and physical well-being. In the event you use any
of the information in this book for yourself, which is your constitutional right,
the author and the publisher assume no responsibility for your actions.

Any people depicted in stock imagery provided by Thinkstock are models,
and such images are being used for illustrative purposes only.
Certain stock imagery © Thinkstock.

Print information available on the last page.

ISBN: 978-1-5043-0209-8 (sc)
ISBN: 978-1-5043-0210-4 (e)

Balboa Press rev. date: 05/18/2016

In memory of Barb

Contents

Introduction

Journey Out of the Fog

From my earliest recollection of learning to read, the fascination of words and the beauty of language has been my passion. Throughout my school education, I developed and refined my skills in many language-related areas. I excelled in literacy-based subjects and languages, becoming an avid reader, public speaker, leader and debater. I enthusiastically engaged in musical theatre and drama, entered writing competitions, and compiled diaries, letters and short stories.

During my work life it was a natural step into a career that drew on and exploited my language skills. This began with adult teaching and expanded to establishing a successful business in career consultation, interview coaching, editing and writing a wide range of business and other documents. This included publishing in a popular small business magazine.

To lose these lifelong, cherished skills to a stroke—in just a few minutes—was devastating: personally and professionally. To know how to regain them was far beyond my comprehension. Shortly after, complicated by obesity and concurrent diagnoses of breast cancer and diabetes, I launched headlong into an intensive project of self-managed recovery. With the insidious nature of all three illnesses, and the enormity of the task, there were no guarantees.

Out of the Fog begins with the lead up to and the occurrence of the stroke, followed by fear and frustration in the immediate aftermath in hospital-based acute stroke services. The subsequent chapters, in a loose chronology, describe an enlightening and sometimes emotional journey of self-help. Surprisingly, along the way I discovered many simple, affordable and unconventional resources around me that I could use as tools in this project.

I realised that my recovery and survival involved a complete lifestyle change. The shock of what that *really* meant—much more than a throwaway line—was the catalyst. As my project accelerated, I began to question society's expectations of older people and the implications for my survival, if I followed the well-worn path into aging.

I learned about my resilience, the necessity of creative thinking, and the value of unconditional support of friends. I also learned how to resist negativism from others that—intentionally or not—accompanies such a massive change and can affect well-established relationships and routines.

The pathways explored in *Out of the Fog* were sometimes planned, and on other occasions appeared from nowhere. They were challenging, frustrating, exhilarating and motivating. They arose largely from intensive self-education, questioning conventional practices, and taking the plunge in unchartered waters.

Out of the Fog puts the consumer in the driver's seat to avoid falling into stereotypical images and behaviours imposed by 'one-size-fits-all' services in a world of convenience, shortcuts and commercially-driven standards. These may not be in everyone's best interest and may even be detrimental to recovery from major illness.

Through a practical approach, *Out of the Fog* raises many questions and provides some solutions for retaining the critical skills that underpin the right to choice, independence, and dignity, through one's life journey.

Come with me on a journey of challenge and adventure….

Alana Henderson

Chapter One

A Very Public Stroke

4.30am: I woke suddenly to the alarm on a day that had begun like many others in the past year. I had worked long into the night, followed by a few hours of restless sleep. I was booked at a client's premises for a full day, working with a recruitment panel. I made some strong coffee, feeling cheated that I had to leave my warm bed for the coldness of my office. With a home-based business, I was quickly working again on a client's unfinished editing job from the previous night, before leaving for the day.

5.40am: I felt tired and agitated, but the warm shower was comforting. Turning my focus to the busy day ahead, I left at 6.00am, grabbing a slice of toast to eat on the way, to begin work by 7.00am. I knew that the highway would be very busy at that time of the morning.

6.40am: Caught in slow-moving traffic, I started to worry that I might be late. I felt irritable and impatient to get out of the long line of cars to reach my destination. Arriving with only a few minutes to spare, I spent the following nine hours in the interview room, with only a brief break for lunch. I used that time to return a few calls to clients. I struggled in the afternoon to think, feeling tired and needing some substantial food and relaxation. But I knew it was unrealistic on that day.

4.00pm: As I prepared to pack up my materials, I felt fatigued—even exhausted—and very hot. I splashed some cool water on my face at the amenities before setting off for home. It briefly occurred to me that as it was winter, I might be coming down with flu. I reminded myself that I didn't have time to be sick. I had to see two clients and complete jobs in my business that night for the looming end-of-financial year. I also had to play piano for a choir rehearsal for two hours. I knew I had to work late or overnight again to complete some urgent jobs before attending another interview panel the next day.

4.45pm: I arrived home and had a quick coffee before I greeted a client for a 5.00pm appointment, and then another at 6.00pm. By this stage I was very tired, irritable, hungry for a decent meal, and anxious about meeting some tight deadlines. I also needed to be at rehearsal within the next hour.

6.45pm: I replied to some emails, made some priority calls, and looked over the list of jobs on my list for that night after rehearsal.

7.20pm: As I ran to the car knowing that I would be late, I drove quickly for the 15-minute trip. My face felt hot and I felt stressed. As I drove, my thoughts were rushing over many things. I told myself several times that I had an impossible night ahead. I became frustrated with the traffic, which was travelling too slowly and the red lights were taking a long time to change. I could feel myself becoming more pressured as I wound through the suburban streets to the practice venue.

7.38pm: I edged my car through the narrow gate and along the few metres to the parking area. As I stopped, I felt extremely hot and began sweating profusely around my face; I wondered if I was getting a bad headache with the pressure I felt in my head. I jumped out of the car, heard the rehearsal underway, and quickly went to the car boot for the music bag. As I lifted the heavy weight onto the cement and slammed down the boot lid, I suddenly heard a strong, rushing wind. I almost dropped the bag, as I felt feverish and dizzy. Within seconds the heat in my head was moving quickly, enveloping my ears, pulsing and filling my head, while the sound of the wind was becoming louder, almost deafening.

I hurried into the room still aware of the wind. I didn't stop to look at the trees around the building—otherwise I might have noticed that they were still. I didn't notice John, the Choir Director, who later told me that he spoke to me as I quickly headed for the stage. Oddly, the sound of the choir voices seemed to be distant, and I was feeling sick.

I dragged the music bag onto the stage and lifted it onto the chair near the piano. In my haste, I fumbled with the zips that wouldn't seem to slide. I couldn't recognise what the choir was singing. I bent down quickly to plug in the light for the piano below the stage, and then grabbed some books from the music bag. I felt faint and agitated, but I was conscious of my lateness. The song finished and the choir members busied themselves finding the next one.

As I sat down to play I gave a quick apology to Margaret, the Conductor. But I couldn't seem to hear my voice. It seemed to be distant from my head, and I felt like I was shouting in the noise of the wind. I didn't hear what she said, but she smiled. I was often running a few minutes late.

I gave a hurried greeting to William, my young assistant and protégé, who grabbed the music books and started organising them for the song list. Through the noise in my head I asked, "What's next on the list?" I didn't hear his response, but he placed the music for 'Annie's Song' on the piano. My head was still pulsing. I expected that I would shortly have a severe headache. I struggled to suppress the feeling and prepared to concentrate on the song.

I began to play at Margaret's signal, but my head felt like it would explode with the heat and the sound of the wind. It was so loud that as I played the introduction I could barely hear the piano. The music on the page seemed unfamiliar. As the choir began to sing, their voices seemed to be coming from another room, yet they were only a few metres away. I felt frustrated and agitated. Suddenly, I became disinterested in the beauty of the music. I couldn't concentrate. *Will this song ever finish?* All I could think about was the pulsing pressure filling my head, ears and face. *What is happening to me?*

As the song finished, I whispered to William, "I can't hear anything. I think I'm getting the flu". He smiled and diligently took over the task of finding the music for the next song. I felt grateful that he was there to help me through the next two hours.

I disciplined myself to work steadily and mechanically through the song list. My thoughts were accelerating and racing from the music to the heat pulsing in my head, to the wind, and to the night ahead at work. I struggled to focus and concentrate on my playing. The songs seemed to be long and the choir didn't seem to be singing them correctly. It was an effort to play a song from start to finish. The sound was jumbled and the music wasn't flowing. I missed a bar of music, then within a few seconds another, then another—and the misses became lengthier.

During the next couple of songs I seemed to be rapidly losing energy. I felt exhausted and I couldn't co-ordinate my playing to keep up with Margaret's conducting. Between songs I said to her, "I can't hear anything". I turned back to the piano to play again. While I knew the music very well after accompanying the choir for many years, it seemed completely unfamiliar. The introductions were too difficult to read and I couldn't count the beats. My eyes wouldn't move smoothly across the page of music. At one stage I realised that I was playing on the wrong part of the keyboard.

William was turning the pages for me, but I couldn't follow the music. As he realised I was lost, a couple of times he pointed to the music to help me. I nervously tried to smile my gratitude at his help. I was becoming frightened.

The songs seemed to finish quickly—too quickly. *Why isn't Margaret doing any repeats of verses and choruses? Concentrate on playing. Get it finished.* I lost my place in the music more frequently, and my anxiety heightened as I realised I now couldn't hear the singers or the piano over the sound in my head. I tried to play louder so I could hear the music, and they could hear what they should be singing. But I became frustrated when it didn't help. At the end of a song, I again whispered to William:

"Was that right?"
"No".

I became completely self-centred. I didn't care what I was playing; I just wanted to finish. I started to play more determinedly, but I was rapidly losing my ability to play. Now the time seemed to drag. My thoughts kept uncontrollably racing to other things, making me lose my place again. I couldn't concentrate on the music. In vain, I desperately tried to regain my composure.

8.10pm: We finished 'Ghost Riders in the Sky'. I had found it almost impossible to keep up the repetitive and tricky left hand in the music, and was aware that I had played badly, out of time, and as if I hadn't seen the music before. I glanced at my watch. *Twenty minutes to coffee break—maybe I should go home to bed.* I had completely lost my comprehension of the music, and as I looked around at the singers, I saw Val looking concerned. I also noticed a group of front row singers looking puzzled. *Why are they looking at me? Was it that bad? I desperately need sleep to get over this flu.*

As the sound of the wind seemed to have dissipated, I felt like I was in a vacuum. Then I became aware of a low but distant burble of sound from the singers. They often chatted between songs, but why were so many of them looking at me? Margaret came quietly to my side. Even without the sound of the wind I could barely hear her speaking. I could see that she was concerned:

"Are you OK? Would you like to conduct and I'll play?"
"No, I'm OK. It's just the flu. I need to go home."

5

Suddenly, John was there in his quiet, calming voice. I could barely hear his voice and it was difficult to understand what he was saying. I became aware that a few other choir members were on the stage near me. Steven was on his phone speaking intently, and relaying his conversation to John, while Sue was kneeling by my chair. She asked me something. But her words were lost. *I have never seen her on the stage before. What is she asking?* "I'm OK. I just need to go home", I repeated. She persevered, gently but firmly. I repeated my attempt at reassurance. I learned later that she was asking me the questions from the Stroke FAST Test that John kept in his wallet.

At least I thought that was what I said. I wasn't sure. I couldn't hear my words. It felt like my mind and my words were out of sync. I couldn't look at people. I felt embarrassed. I wanted everyone to leave me alone and just let me go home. Margaret was there again, reassuring me. I heard John speak to me and I caught the word "ambulance."

I panicked. *An ambulance?* I became irritated. I firmly repeated, "I'm OK. I just need to go home". I wanted to be away from the attention. I wanted to be home in the safety and warmth of my bed. *I certainly don't need an ambulance! A couple of hours of sleep will fix everything.*

I turned around to the music bag to get my car keys. They weren't there. I fumbled in the top pocket of the bag. *They must be here.* My irritation was turning into anger towards myself. *How could I lose my keys now? Where could they possibly be? How silly must I look in front of 60 people?* Unbeknown to me, Margaret had discreetly removed them from the music bag to delay my intended departure.

People spoke to me calmly and gently. "I'm OK. I just need to go home", I repeated. I didn't seem to be able to say anything else. I wasn't sure what I was saying. They didn't seem to hear or understand me. *If I insist they'll understand. Am I really speaking clearly? Better for me to go home and get away from this scene.*

All rational thought had left me. I didn't care if I left the bag or the music, I just needed to find the keys and drive home. I couldn't think of anything beyond going home to bed. I couldn't think about returning to playing the piano. The heavy feeling in my head and face was overwhelming. My mind seemed muddled. I tried to force myself to follow my thoughts clearly. People were kind but persistent. Still on the stage, I felt thoroughly self-conscious in front of the group. John, bending near me, said in a calm voice:

"The ambulance is on its way. We'll just check everything's OK."
"Well, I'll go out and wait for them outside."

I was in a panic. *All I have is the flu*! I didn't want to alarm the singers, but it was obviously too late.

I tried to stand up, but I felt weak. My legs felt disconnected from my body. They felt like they could barely move and my joints wouldn't work properly when I walked. My hands felt swollen and stiff. I thought I would fall. Suddenly, people were beside me, watching me, speaking around me, and helping me to walk to the front door. I tried to hear what they were saying, but the sounds were like a low murmur, with unintelligible babble. *Are they talking to me, or to each other? What's wrong with my legs?*

I looked back and saw William standing anxiously near the piano, and asked Helen to take him home. *Did she hear me, or understand me?* I couldn't tell. I thought she nodded to me.

They guided me to a chair just outside the door to wait for the ambulance. I felt embarrassed; the centre of attention for all the wrong reasons. People were speaking to me in reassuring tones, but I gave up trying to understand them. They didn't seem to understand what I was saying. *Why won't they listen to me?* Sue knelt near me and touched me gently on the arm.

I was now completely self-absorbed with my racing and panicking thoughts. *I'll get the ambulance out of the way, and then I'll go home. I can take care of myself. I'll come back next week, over the flu. Why do they think there's something wrong with me? I can handle the flu.*

Within a few minutes, the ambulance arrived and carefully negotiated the vehicle into the little courtyard where I was sitting. The paramedic approached me with a kindly face and an easy smile. He crouched in front of me and I tried to tell him that I was OK. He worked quickly and reassuringly while he took some observations. He asked me some questions, but I couldn't understand him. I told him that I was OK. I was vaguely aware of him giving me an injection. I saw his colleague lifting the stretcher out of the back of the van. *What's that for? Why do I need that? I'm not going to hospital! I have too much to do at home!*

I was feeling very weak, unable to resist their gentle insistence. They quickly and efficiently helped me onto the stretcher, and within 15 minutes I was in the Emergency Department in hospital.

I didn't know how long I sat with the paramedic in the corridor. I stopped trying to talk to him, as I couldn't follow what he said. I was conscious of continually asking him to repeat himself. I fought to stay awake, aware of increasing drowsiness, but desperate for sleep. Then I was wheeled into a small cubicle. People came and went frequently, speaking to me and taking observations. I could barely hear what they said. They seemed to speak too quickly. I dozed several times. Then a familiar face appeared—a nurse client that I knew from my business—but I couldn't remember her name. I was very drowsy, frightened and disorientated in a completely unfamiliar environment. *What is happening to me? How can I get home? Where is my car?* All reason and rational thought had gone.

I wanted to call Heather, my close friend. I knew she would help me. I indicated to the nurse that I needed to write and she gave me a piece of paper and a pen. My hands didn't seem to work properly as I struggled to close my fingers around the pen. I shakily wrote down her first name, but I tried in vain for several minutes to think of her surname. *If only I could stay awake to think!* I was frustrated and frantic. I tried repeatedly to remember the name of her workplace. Finally, I partially wrote down a few letters and the nurse recognised

Heather's name. I was very grateful to the nurse, because I couldn't think clearly about anything.

Sleep quickly enveloped me again. I heard a nurse mention, "scan". I woke from my drowsiness, and as I was wheeled out of the ED, I briefly saw two familiar but anxious faces: Vanessa (William's mother) and her sister Lyndal. I wanted to call out to them to help me—but I didn't have the energy to speak. I felt alone and lost.

I was wheeled rapidly to a large room and quickly assisted into a hospital gown. Through my 'deafness' I heard the hammering of the scanning machine. The nurse was reassuring as I tried to move and keep my eyes focused. I was fighting sleep, but losing the battle. I felt like I was sinking slowly into deep, calm water. I couldn't think from one minute to the next.

Sometime later, I woke momentarily, conscious of someone in the room. I saw two people in blue operating theatre uniforms standing at the end of the bed. Again I panicked. *I must have a brain tumour! I must be going for an operation!* My brain shut down. As I drifted in and out of sleep, I didn't know that Heather had arrived.

I woke again as I became aware that I was being wheeled down a corridor. We arrived in a dimly-lit room and I was helped into bed. The sheets felt cold but I fell asleep within seconds, thoroughly exhausted.

Chapter Two

Surviving the Health Juggernaut

I woke at dawn and lay still for a few seconds. I was aware of the strangeness of the room, the silence around me, and the early morning light slowly creeping through the window. Remembering the two blue-uniformed staff from the previous night in the ED, I cautiously felt my head—no bandages. I felt numb. *They mustn't have been able to do the operation. I must be dying. Will I die today? How could this be happening to me?* Then I slept again. I was vaguely aware of someone taking observations in the dim light. But I couldn't wake up.

The next time I woke, the room was brighter and I was aware of noises in the corridor outside the room. A nurse briefly came in and took more observations. She didn't look at me or speak to me. I couldn't seem to organise my thoughts quickly enough to ask her what was happening to me, before she left the room. *Why can't I speak?* I didn't realise that I had lost the ability to speak coherently.

Alone, I tried to think clearly, calmly and rationally. But my brain felt scrambled and black. I couldn't think logically. *Am I dreaming? I need to get home. I have to be at work. Why am I still here? I'll be late.* But I felt weak and drowsy and my limbs felt heavy. I didn't know if I could move.

Needing to go to the bathroom, I carefully sat up, and cautiously moved my legs around to sit on the side of the bed for a few seconds. As I stepped out onto the floor, I almost fell. My legs seemed disjointed, numbed, disconnected from my body, and incapable of holding my weight. I steadied myself on the bed and stood up slowly, but my hands felt strange. I moved them but they felt like they were in thick gloves, swollen and slow to move. I managed to stagger to and from the bathroom in the room—holding onto the wall and furniture—then again sought the comfort and warmth of the bed. I slept again.

Then Heather arrived. I was so pleased and relieved to see her. We had been good friends for many years and I knew she would help me. She said quietly, "You've had a stroke, a cerebral haemorrhage". I felt so relieved—even elated! *No brain tumour! I'm not dying! I can cope with a stroke!*

Realising that I wouldn't get to work, I struggled to remember the name of my client's personal assistant, for Heather to let her know what had happened. When I tried to talk and explain what had to be done, I was shocked as I stumbled, stammered and only managed a few fractured words. I tried to tell her about my legs and hands. But my words seemed muffled and jumbled.

My mind was in such turmoil. I felt frustrated and angry that I couldn't think clearly or remember names. Eventually, after several exasperating attempts, I remembered some semblance of my client's name. I used gestures to indicate that I needed something to write on, so I could communicate more easily. Heather left to make the call.

When she returned, she brought with her a blue folder containing a large writing pad, and some toiletries in a little bag. She assured me that she would be back later in the day. I knew that I could rely on her to sort things out for me.

Motivated by her visit, I immediately began to think about what to do to help myself. I started trying to remember people's names that I needed to contact: clients, staff, friends, and suppliers to my business. It was extremely difficult to think of first names, even though I could see their faces in my mind, and I couldn't remember any surnames.

Although I tried for several minutes, it sapped my energy. I worried how I could remember things I needed to do, such as urgent jobs for my business, if I couldn't think of names. I couldn't concentrate for more than a few seconds, flitting from one thought to another. *How will I ever do my job again? Will I ever play piano again?*

I sought refuge in sleep to build some energy and get on with the task. I woke a short time later and now felt less apprehensive. I told myself to be disciplined and determined, so that I could overcome this situation and return home as quickly as possible—at the most—a few days. I had no idea about the severity of the stroke, the implications, the risks or how to deal with it. But I knew I was resilient!

During that first day I met several Health Professionals (HPs). A nurse accompanied me to the shower. I knew this was essential for safety, and I accepted it without question or resistance. Nevertheless, I found it very embarrassing to be naked in the shower, being watched by a stranger. So I showered, dried and dressed myself as quickly as I could. I carefully walked the few steps to the bathroom mirror and proceeded to pull out some items from the toiletry bag to place them on the narrow shelf.

The nurse squeezed some toothpaste onto the brush and handed it to me. I smiled at her and gestured that the shelf was full. I momentarily held the toothbrush lightly on my head, as an attempt at humour, to relieve my feeling of awkwardness. There was no response. I completed the task as quickly as possible.

> *Medical File Entry:*
> *'She was compulsive and 'flighty' during showering and dressing. Given toothbrush and toothpaste to clean teeth but patient commenced to clean her hair with same instead.'*

(When I read this comment in my medical file several weeks later, I was annoyed that I had been described so insensitively. Her entry was at odds with the initial written assessment stating, 'She was orientated to her surroundings'. She completely disregarded the fact, that a few minutes earlier, I had completed all personal tasks unassisted. I thought about how easy it was for HPs to have no accountability for their comments in a patient's file. I was saddened that there was no room for a light-hearted moment in stroke services).

A young person wearing a stethoscope (I presumed she was a medical student) came into the room. She gave no greeting or introduction, and busied herself in performing what seemed to be a never-ending list of observations. She was preoccupied with her notes, worked nervously, frequently wrung her hands, spoke to herself and often sighed in frustration. I wanted to assist her with her observations, but my brain couldn't form the words to ask her anything about her tasks.

Her body language showed her exasperation in repeating some tasks when she didn't seem to be happy with the outcome. I didn't know what I could do to help her. Through the entire list she gave me no eye contact, didn't seek my co-operation at any time, ask any questions, or explain any task she was about to perform. She just did it. Nor did she thank me for my co-operation as she left the room.

She left me feeling bleak and sad. Her lack of common courtesy at a time when I was in shock and very fragile, left me feeling like I was an inconvenience to her in her job. I felt valueless.

A physiotherapist assessed my mobility. On her direction, I moved carefully out of the bed to take a short walk outside the room. My legs were unco-ordinated. To avoid falling, I steadied myself on the furniture and the wall to complete the test. I walked slowly and tried as hard as I could, so that my staggering didn't appear to be a big problem. She didn't ask me about the feeling in my legs or comment to me on my physical difficulty. I didn't tell her about my hands that felt swollen, fearing that this might delay my discharge.

Medical File Entry:
'? (Sic) vision field loss of spatial awareness reduced as tending to run into objects and doorways.'

(This was poor judgment and an incorrect assessment of the cause of my difficulty with walking. Regardless, it was never followed up).

When alone, I walked frequently around my room carefully and slowly—continually bending and moving my legs, knees, ankles, wrists and finger joints—to regain my mobility and sensitivity. (Within two or three days, I could walk almost normally, but the lack of feeling in my hands took several weeks to completely disappear).

A speech therapist was friendly and business-like in her approach as she immediately began assessing my language skills. I initially felt at ease with her greeting, expecting that she might explain what she would do. She immediately gave me a range of strange questions, some of which I answered relatively easily with single words, but I quickly became frustrated. I had no idea of what she was trying to test, nor did she offer an explanation. I felt a sense of urgency for her to test what I knew or had lost—the language relevant to my life. From her facial expression I knew I was failing her questions. It made me feel patronised, humiliated and frightened.

With growing panic, my mind rapidly became blank, and I was disheartened that I had failed miserably. My mind was running into brick walls that stopped my words, and it became harder to respond. My known level of understanding and comprehension of language had deserted me.

She knew nothing about my background for many years as an adult educator, public speaker and editor, or the need for and style of language skills needed when working with a wide-ranging client base. I felt discouraged. The more I tried, the more I failed.

I couldn't ask her why this type of assessment was necessary. (I learned later that using childlike language references in assessments was standard practice). As my tension rose, my language turned to gibberish or was non-existent when I tried to speak. I was devastated at the possibility that I couldn't return to my work. I felt that her assessment was completely irrelevant to my language and my life.

She left with no indication of what I needed, she didn't talk to me about a plan for how my language might recover or offer any reassurance about anything in my future. *Have I lost all capacity for language as an adult? Is there something 'magical' in simplistic and childlike questions? Am I now reduced to an infant level of language for communication?* I felt that I was a lost cause. I despaired that I might never know how to communicate in 'my world' again. I quickly began to lose hope in my ability to overcome this situation, while I remained in this environment. I desperately wanted to leave as quickly as possible, and do what I could to help myself.

Heather returned later that day, followed shortly after by Annette, the other Choir Director. When trying hard to talk to them coherently, I became more aware of my real impairment, because they came from my world—not the unfamiliar environment of the HPs. As far as I was concerned, this was the authentic baseline assessment for my language. (From my own experience as an educator, I knew that adults want to know that what they do or learn has relevance to their life. They are experts at determining what is important for them as individuals.)

I was desperate to appear OK, so my friends could support me to go home. But in trying to talk to them, I became fearful about the long road ahead. It was as if I had never spoken English fluently. Although I knew what I needed to learn, I realised that it would take me more than a few days to recover, as I had suggested to Heather earlier that day. They were respectful, supportive and confident that things could improve. There was genuineness in the way they spoke to me, and their warmth gave me some hope. I felt fortunate and grateful to have two highly successful leaders in these women as my advocates. It occurred to me that with Heather and Annette I felt positive, but with the HPs—the experts—I felt a sense of hopelessness.

From the moment they left, the writing pad in the blue folder became my communication line, my recovery tool and my precious diary. I knew that I couldn't verbally communicate easily, but I could write down my observations in single words and short phrases for my questions for HPs. At that stage, I didn't know that I couldn't write fluently in full sentences. My expertise in taking notes as a scribe in my business was sufficient for me to record the information I needed, albeit now in scratched notes, with many errors.

I began in earnest in retrieving the skills that were relevant to me. I needed to know if they could be recovered at all. I began to write a list of names that I could practise aloud to prove to myself that I could learn to speak again. I was more organised and motivated than my effort earlier that morning.

I started with single-syllable names matched to faces that I could visualise: 'Barb', 'John', 'Frank', 'Pam', 'Nance', 'Pat' and 'Ruth'. I wrote them down so I could read them, and practise them correctly. I quickly realised that I couldn't remember any surnames, although I had known all of the people on my list for many years. With short bursts of seconds of repetition, visualising their faces one at a time, I found I could say at least a few names, slowly and accurately.

Later that night, I tried and failed with a few two-syllable names: 'Lynda', 'Winsome', 'Nina', 'Robert', 'Jackie', 'Wendy' and 'Andrew'. The list in my diary shows that 'Annette' was written as 'Anated' and 'Bernard' as 'Berladine.' I congratulated myself at my recognition that I had written them *incorrectly*. But it took my brain some time to correct them.

When Frank, my Business Manager and his wife Carol visited me, I struggled with Bernard's name. Frank helped me to pronounce it several times, but I couldn't spontaneously get the rhythm without multiple attempts. I still couldn't pronounce his name when he visited a few days later.

In those early days—when I was so desperate to know what I could do to help myself—none of the HPs mentioned the stroke directly to me or gave me an explanation, plan, counselling or any spark of hope that I had a future. I quickly got the message that trying to speak with HPs for any purpose, except to respond to their questions, was useless—even an irritation.

So I began practising day and night; every waking moment that I was alone. My expertise in short naps enabled me to sleep little, and work hard, over a few hours. In my diary, I set up exercises working from single words e.g. 'red', 'blue', 'sing', 'Skype', to three-word phrases, e.g. (describing the flower arrangements in my room) 'beautiful orange lilies' and 'gorgeous yellow jonquils' to regain some rhythm and intonation in my language. I began to recover a few words more confidently.

When I couldn't find the right word, sometimes it came to me later and stayed with me. At those times, I felt like a little piece of information had fallen back correctly into its pathway in my brain. But at other times, thoughts came into my mind and just as quickly disappeared. In those instances, I had no recollection of what I had been thinking during previous minutes. But I told myself that I was very slowly mending the fractures in my brain that seemed to be in a million pieces. I frequently reminded myself that with my determination, if I could repair one fracture, I could repair a thousand!

I thought through procedures in my office, such as processing client emails, taking telephone calls, filing documents and processing accounts—familiar procedures I had used for years. I tried to think through the procedures systematically and faltered many times. Each time, I started again. I started with the first couple of steps in my mind, slowly recited them, forced my brain to think coherently, and then slowly added the next steps to accurately complete the procedure. I tired easily. Just when I thought I had remembered a lengthy procedure after several attempts—I often forgot it just as quickly. Others randomly stayed in my vocabulary and memory.

During my continual practice, I became aware that my skills in manipulating numbers were also affected. I mentioned this problem to a speech therapist. She seemed more attuned to my frustration than the other HPs. During one session, we practised together counting numbers in sequence. With her help after a shaky start, I counted numbers correctly up to ten.

But I wasn't satisfied. I asked about calculations, not just counting. She gave me a few sheets of graded maths calculations that I attempted a few minutes after she left. I easily completed some simple calculations. But as I tried some more complex calculations with multiples, they were meaningless. I couldn't remember how to use simple addition and subtraction procedures. This gave me some idea of my level of numeracy, to at least perform basic accounting relevant to my business. For the rest, I could use a calculator.

For me, I realised that this was the baseline, so I began working with multiples and inventing calculations to re-acquaint myself with more complex numbers. I was desperate to salvage any glimmer of hope. This was at least a small step forward.

While Sandy was visiting, a speech therapist arrived and asked me some safety questions:

> "What would you do if you arrived home and your front door was open?"
> "My little dog would be out and about to visit his friends, so I'd leave the door and the gate open for him to come home."

Sandy and I laughed—we knew my little dog was an 'escapee'! The HP didn't share our joke. I realised I had failed again. And there was no option for me to repeat my response. The damage was done. After she left, realising that my attempt at humour had counted against me, I spent a long time making a list of safety procedures in my diary that indicated how I could be safe at home. When I showed them to her at the next visit, she dismissed the pages with a cursory glance, with no recognition of their value. Again I felt a surge of hopelessness.

I had shown the capacity, through my own effort, to construct and link a list of simple activities into a sequence—at least to follow written instructions—far beyond her assessment. Surely this was positive! But her response left me feeling that I had made a false assumption about my ability to do simple activities to help myself.

The HP had no concept of how valuable this tool was to me. I knew I could transfer this methodology for learning a task to many others such as personal activities, following lists in a daily diary, or implementing procedures in my business. *Why is it wrong or useless?*

> *Medical File entry:*
> *'Able to follow 1-step simple commands. Unable to follow 2-step commands.'*

(From this report in my medical file, there was no mention that I had any functional skills beyond her assessment. Instead, there was a preoccupation with recognising two-dimensional pictures of objects that I found useless to my life).

There was no understanding from the HPs that in a state of shock and fear of what the future held for me, they needed to give me some motivation—some inspiration, some lifeline, some hope—to work with them. I needed to believe and trust in them and their skills. But a smiled greeting and a courteous approach were not sufficient to gain this trust. I needed to see relevance in their work with me.

My apparent failure in response to what I saw as useless assessments, quickly cemented a feeling of powerlessness and frustration.

I tried again. For the speech therapist's next visit, I wrote two pages of simple notes called, 'My Lifecycle Activities' and how they should be done. I listed the friends and local services that could support me at home. It took me hours to compile the list. It was ignored.

From my many clients in the health industry, I knew that safety was an obsession among HPs. To convince them that I could go home, I spent a long time thinking about and writing the procedure for a favourite but simple cauliflower soup recipe. It meant safely using a stove. It took me a long time to write the 14 steps, one-by-one, in a logical order. This was the result (complete with errors) in my diary:

1. Turn the hot plate, high
2. Splash olive oil in the pot
3. Peel 1 onion, rough
4. ~~Sorter~~ saute for 3-4 minutes
5. Chop cauliflower small ~~in to flowers/small~~ into bits
6. In olive oil for 3-4 minutes
7. Stock ~~member~~ powder, 3 teaspoons
8. Water 2 cups
9. Milk 2 cups
10. Simmer for 15 minutes
11. Let it cool for 2 minutes ~~from~~ away from stove
12. Sender to blender in batches, in a larger bowl to smooth
13. In a low ~~setter~~ setting, ~~stirred~~ in philly cream till ~~smost~~ smooth
14. ~~Usy~~ Use fresh ~~b~~herbs.

This simple recipe showed, that by taking my time, I could write logically and prioritise tasks. I wanted to show the therapist how I could use this system to reconstruct many skills in my life, and be safe and independent at home even without language. She dismissed my writing.

My pride in the achievement of carefully writing down the method in detail with only a few errors—mostly that I recognised and corrected—was dashed by her response.

Over many years in my work as an adult educator, I had used Bloom's Taxonomy: classic educational principles and an excellent model for teaching, to assess and promote higher order thinking. I knew that as a result of the stroke I had fallen from the top level of the Taxonomy that I used in my work, to the lowest, often identified with people with limited literacy and poor understanding of how to apply knowledge and complex concepts.

This was evident in the ensuing days, when I felt miserable, stressed or angry at the HPs. I thought many times about leaving the hospital. But at that level of cognitive functioning, I couldn't think clearly to plan the logistics and the consequences of making complex decisions. *How can I leave the hospital? What will happen to me? Will I have another stroke? How will I get away without being seen? What will happen to the clothes that Heather and Annette have bought for me? What will happen to my beautiful flowers? Will they drag me back? How will I find the front door of the ward without being noticed?* These illogical and random thoughts surged over me in waves many times in the first few days, and continually plagued my mind. They frequently kept me awake and were too difficult for me to solve without the capacity for logical thinking.

There were constant frustrations. I wrote the name of the Taxonomy in my diary so speech therapists could make no mistake about what I meant, rather than confuse them with my fractured words. But they looked at the note in my diary and each considered it to be irrelevant, saying, "I don't know anything about it".

Knowing that there were big gaps in my cognitive processes, I was desperate for them to help me to move through them again to my pre-stroke skills, as quickly as possible. But I was puzzled. How could people who are retraining adults, not know about Bloom's Taxonomy? By realising where I was on the Taxonomy, I knew I could retrain myself using my own resources, as I had done for years with my clients. The urgency to leave hospital became foremost in my mind.

A dichotomy quickly emerged. On one hand, my visitors treated me normally, regardless of my brain injury. I welcomed them and felt comforted by their support. They treated me respectfully, letting me stumble without making me feel that I was failing or fearing judgment by my attempts. We often laughed at my gobbledygook, and their visits became my practical therapy sessions. I tried harder to improve myself during our conversations without feeling self-conscious. I made many errors in my language, but in fits and starts

I slowly became better at recognising them. When I realised I had said wrong words, sometimes I could correct them. When I tried to speak at a normal pace, I often unknowingly used incorrect and incoherent words.

On the other hand, with the HPs I felt like I was being watched, judged and criticised. I was on edge at all times in their presence, fearing that failing their tests might keep me longer in hospital. They didn't indicate what they were testing me for, which left me annoyed. With every interaction with them my sense of loss and hopelessness grew. The negative, pessimistic, and frequent judgemental comments throughout my medical file, attests to the lack of expectation of the HPs about my potential to understand anything they said.

I frequently experienced what I termed 'black holes', when I couldn't speak for a few seconds if my brain couldn't find the word at all. In my mind I could see an impenetrable blackness. This fracturing of my language left me anxious and frustrated. On one occasion, I suggested to Annette that with my new language of jumbled words, I could have a career in stand-up comedy!

The chatter of my visitors made me think about how to improve the way I communicated in the different languages of friendship, business and music. I had always moved seamlessly between various types of communication in the course of a day, but now I struggled to get even the simplest sentences together in a coherent way in the right context. My visitors became my real therapists.

I had a growing and frightening realisation that many HPs considered that loss of language equalled loss of intelligence. They disregarded my use of my diary for my own therapy as futile and irrelevant. What they missed was that I could see, respond to my surroundings and write down my observations, even in short notes. They showed no interest in my effort or what I saw as useful skills. For those who wrote in my file that I was doing 'homework'—they assumed on direction of HPs—was completely false. No HPs looked at my work in any depth to see what it comprised. It was my own work, my own strategies developed from a sense of desperation to do something of value for myself.

Strangely, when alone, I knew that I could *think perfectly* through sentences, but the transfer to actual words in conversation was where I faltered with frequent mistakes. My many years as a scribe in my business meant that I knew how to paraphrase language into significant written phrases and words. I seemed to still have this skill to some degree, so it became the basis for my copious diary entries.

I drew on these skills to develop a strategy of writing a phrase or several words to remind me what I wanted to communicate with HPs. As I couldn't write sentences fully, I taught myself to *think* what I wanted to say, then immediately write a trigger—a word or phrase—to remember it when trying to speak. I set up sections of my writing pad so I didn't forget the information that I wanted to mention, discuss or question with specific HPs. I saw this technique as a communication strategy for the few minutes that might be available to talk with them. They repeatedly dismissed my questions.

I learned, quite by accident, that if I put a line through each word or phrase as I used it, my eye would naturally fall to the next empty space below. This assisted me to focus, concentrate and write down the next note.

But as the HPs relentlessly—intentionally or not—chipped away at my resistance to their assembly line processes, I could see my hope slipping further away. It was such a tiring struggle to fight the battle. Perhaps desensitisation to the needs of individuals resulted in them consistently ignoring my efforts at self-help and their reluctance to explain anything about what they were doing.

I feared losing the strength that had always given me resilience and self-confidence to overcome life's challenges. I felt there was disregard for me as a thinking, functional person. My brain injury should not have diminished their respect for me as a patient, yet it clearly underpinned their attitude and behaviour. I noticed that from HPs in every discipline that I encountered, there were barriers placed on my direct input into my recovery, unless it was on their terms or their request. The battle that ensued manifested itself in their behaviour in loss of empathy and respect for me, increasing my frustration with every encounter.

I quickly realised that regardless of my intuitive needs, non-compliance from the patient was to be reined in to meet the needs of the system in meeting its quality standards and completing the check boxes. There was no attempt to collaborate with me, and no plan for my individual needs, aside from the conventional one-size-fits-all structure that characterised this environment. If there was a plan, as mentioned sporadically in my medical file, it was never discussed with me, or anywhere to be found, when I read the file several weeks later. What value was a plan with no input from the person—the subject of the plan—who was capable and keen to participate?

Like an unstoppable juggernaut, the patient had to fit the system or was discarded and ignored. In this unhelpful and uncaring environment, the HPs' perceptions of my behaviour and recovery were distorted or adjusted for convenience in meeting the requirements of the system. This resulted in many inaccurate, careless and untrue statements in reports in my medical file.

> *Medical File entry:*
> *'… new onset of dysphagia… expressive and receptive dysphagia…'*

(Dysphagia, difficulty with swallowing, was never evident. The entire nonsensical report, written by a doctor—based on a spelling error or ignorance—is permanently lodged in my file. Clearly this HP had not read the previous notes. As there were no amendments in the file, perhaps no-one else noticed the error).

I treated the HPs courteously and in a friendly manner, because of fear of repercussions and negative assessments. But I needed some inspiration from them to know that I could recover my life. But not one HP gave me any glimmer of hope at any time. After their 'care',

I was often overcome by misery at my predicament and felt powerless to change the situation after apparently failing everything.

Although their body language and behaviour had told me much at the time, afterwards when I read my file, I felt vindicated in my belief that the various HPs had a very narrow and limited assessment of my skills. There was no room for lateral thinking, creativity or recognition of the patient's effort or willingness to contribute to their own recovery. It was clearly seen as irrelevant and not worth reporting. Yet the file is full of inaccurate assessments and assumptions about the loss of my skills at the time.

Several junior doctors tested me with what I called the 'Peter Rabbit Test'. An undiagnosed auditory processing disorder meant that I frequently missed the verbal cues and found it difficult to follow their directions, especially if they weren't in my visual field. But I quickly learned, that if people faced me at a distance of about a metre, and spoke clearly, I could understand most of what they said, and comply with their request.

On one occasion, a doctor came rushing into the room, threw the chart down and stood at the end of the bed. "Remove your glasses, (blah, blah, blah)", he barked. I got the first part, but had no idea about the rest of his direction. My fractured brain could not process his speech quickly or from that distance.

He was obviously in a rush, so I complied immediately and removed my glasses. I wanted to appear co-operative even though I didn't know what he wanted. With my severe short-sightedness, I could barely see the movement of his wiggling fingers, held up on both sides of his head. I assumed that he wanted me to look towards the finger movement. He grabbed his chart as he ran out of the room, saying, "No, not good enough to go home yet!" I had failed again. This was repeated on all other attempts through ignorance of the task on my part, and lack of communication on theirs. But what did I fail? What did this test mean? Why did I have to remove my glasses to do the test? He showed no consideration or recognition that my auditory processing had slowed with the stroke. While various doctors performed this test several times, this was the only one that directed me to remove my glasses. I still don't know why.

I wanted the HPs to listen to what I was asking, and honestly answer my questions. *When can I go home? When can I speak to The Doctor who will send me home? When does he visit? Will I be able to play piano again?* In desperation, in my fractured words, I asked everyone who came in the room: nurses, doctors, therapists, cleaners and volunteers. Their answer was always the same, "I don't know. You'll have to wait". *Wait, for what? What aren't they telling me? Was there more damage from the stroke than I thought?* Perhaps the specific answers were difficult, but they weren't impossible, and they could have been delivered in more positive terms. But their vague and patronising attitude, bereft of any detail, convinced me that I had lost my intelligence, along with my language. With each interaction I felt more powerless and devalued. My hope and self-esteem faded.

At one stage, I was sitting in bed writing in my diary, with my knees up to prevent me sliding down the bed. A nurse backed into the room holding a catheter bag and tube. She paused for a few seconds as she spoke to someone else in a similar uniform, leaning on the doorway. Still in conversation with her colleague, she turned and walked over to the bed, and pulled the blankets back. There was no greeting, warning, education or explanation to me about the procedure or expectation of the sensation of being catheterised.

I was mortified at this unexpected and brutal invasion of my privacy. I froze. My brain shut down to blackness. Within seconds, and with practised efficiency, she lodged the catheter in place, like fitting a key neatly into a lock. She kept up her conversation with her colleague. Suddenly I felt myself wetting the bed. I was ashamed and embarrassed, unable to stop it happening. I couldn't speak.

The procedure finished, she took her sample and left me sitting in the wet bed, completely exposed. She joined her colleague in the corridor, and they continued their conversation as they walked away. I panicked. *How can I change the bed? How will I explain this to the nurses?* I carefully moved out of the bed and felt for the wet sheet. It was dry.

Then I felt angry. I was outraged at this disregard for my dignity. I felt like a piece of meat, to be manipulated and discarded. The anxiety caused by this procedure could have been allayed by a simple explanation. *If she was here to check if I was bleeding from the neck, she didn't do that either—because she didn't look above my navel!*

One morning, I woke feeling nauseous and hot. *Some cool water on my face might help.* I went to the bathroom but the water didn't help. As I stood at the basin I suddenly felt faint. I quickly sat down on the toilet, pressed the nurses' call button, and grabbed the side rails to prevent me falling. I rested my head against the cistern with my eyes closed. Shortly after, I heard the door open and a voice said, "Oh, it's only a patient, she looks like she's dead". And the door closed.

I panicked and tried to get out of the bathroom, desperately not wanting to die in a toilet. Still seeing coloured lights before a faint, I fell through the door onto the floor in my giddiness. Two nurses lifted me onto a shower chair and rapidly wheeled me into my room. They worked swiftly to check my blood pressure, remove the pillow and administer oxygen. Then they left the room and after several minutes, the nausea and giddiness started to subside.

Then two nurses walked in and stood at the bedside, looking down at me. One referred to my single room near the nurses' desk (I recognised the same voice from the bathroom):

"So why's she in this room anyway?"
"She's a nice lady, but she might take off. So we have to watch her."

I wanted to scream at them—I'm alive! I'm a person! But I felt weak, my language deserted me and I felt like I was already dead. They proceeded to converse with each other while they made the bed around me, then left the room with no further interaction with me. My fall through the bathroom door onto the floor was not reported in my file. Yet two nurses came from several metres away to help me from the floor into the chair to be taken back to my room. The brief reference to the incident in my medical file was inaccurate.

The next evening, an event* occurred which caused me to be very afraid for my physical safety. Heather dealt with the issue following hospital policy to prevent recurrence. I felt reassured by her actions. But my anxiety was at the maximum and I was desperate to leave for the safety and protection of my home.

Later that night, a nurse finally said, "The Doctor will see you in the morning". I clung to the hope of a meeting with The Doctor as the only way to be authorised home as quickly as possible.

I walked around in my room, all night till dawn, practising what I had to say to him. I was afraid that if I slept I wouldn't be able to remember what I had practised. I knew I needed to appear confident and capable in order to negotiate with him about going home. I repeatedly rehearsed word-for-word what to say, to plead with him. I could hear my language becoming more confident and coherent.

During the long, dark hours I often practised at the window. I watched two helicopters arrive, and wondered about the jobs of people that I saw walking around the grounds. I kept going over and over my words for The Doctor.

No-one came into the room until around 2.30am (I noticed the time on the wall near the nurses' station outside my room). A nurse opened the door and looked startled when she saw me leaning against the wall at the end of the bed. "Oh!" she said, and immediately closed the door. If she had observed the room at that time, she would have noticed that my bed was undisturbed.

I resumed practising my plea to The Doctor the following morning.

> *Medical File Entry*: (4.00am)
> '... *settled and sleeping...*'

---

* personal details omitted

I noticed the world forming into recognisable shapes outside the window of my room at dawn, far later than 4.00am. I lay down exhausted on the bed with the intention of waking after a short nap. But I fell into a deeper sleep.

"Wake up! Wake up! The Doctor's here!" yelled a nurse, waking me suddenly. And he was walking into the room followed by his team.

Drowsy, barely awake and still exhausted from a night without sleep, I knew I looked dishevelled and groggy. I tried to tell him what I had practised for hours, but my language quickly deserted me. Desperate to explain my need to go home—to plead with him—I quickly broke down. I became extremely distressed and angry with myself that I couldn't coherently plead my case. I felt tension in my chest and I could barely breathe.

I felt vulnerable, out of control and embarrassed in front of the entire team of HPs. I was only interested in speaking to The Doctor at the time on very private issues. There was no discussion or choice about whether I would be willing to be observed by a large group, especially when in a highly distressed state. As a matter of respect for the patient, why wouldn't the onlookers leave the room?

The Doctor was clearly annoyed with me, and with a flip of his hand he said in an irritated manner to his team, "She's too emotional, she needs a social worker!" He then stood briefly at the end of the bed looking in my direction. He muttered behind his hand to another doctor, before walking out of the room. I was completely distraught and humiliated by this behaviour. He showed no interest in dealing with my concerns. I felt like a weak and pitiful zoo exhibit being watched by a crowd.

I had lost my chance to convince him that I had to go home. With all the hours of practice, I had failed.

On his next visit with his team I tried a different strategy. I was more rested, standing away from the bed, hair combed, wearing my dressing gown, trying to look more confident, calm and capable. Still angry about his previous response to me, I immediately told him, very carefully and as clearly as I could, that I wouldn't accept his disrespectful attitude again. I slowly explained how I had continuously worked very hard from 12 hours after my stroke, and had made noticeable improvements to improve my language skills. I wanted him to understand the insight I had into my stroke, and the gains I had made. He didn't respond.

Realising that he was disinterested, I persisted and urged him to give me a benchmark so that I could prove to him that I was ready to go home. His response was, "A benchmark? A benchmark?" Then he left the room. That was the last time I ever spoke with The Doctor.

I was outraged that I had been treated with such contempt, and humiliated twice in front of the team of HPs. I didn't care if he didn't like me, or didn't smile at me—but as a patient, I had the right to be treated with respect. His attitude was mirrored by the HPs at every level that showed similar behaviour.

Another doctor later showed me the scan of my brain haemorrhage in a genuine effort to explain to me why it was important for me to stay in hospital. I thanked her for her courtesy but reinforced my need to go home. While she showed some awareness of my frustration, she was powerless to move beyond the juggernaut's relentless and destructive force.

Next day, a social worker visited me. Aside from introducing herself she gave me no indication of her function. *Is she here to act as an advocate on my behalf to The Doctor? This is my chance!* I grasped the opportunity to speak with her and proceeded to pour out my heart to this young woman. *Can she have any empathy with me? She seems so young. I have no choice but to seize the moment.*

I spoke as clearly and slowly as I could, so she could make no mistake about the urgency for me to go home. I told her very personal details from my life that I had never disclosed to anyone else. I wanted her to understand how I was resilient and capable of looking after myself. She asked me very little. *Is this the way these HPs operate?* Her silence gave me no clues as to what I should be telling her. This spurred me to keep talking so she could argue assertively on my behalf when talking to The Doctor. I told her anything I could think of to assist me.

At times I fought back the tears at my embarrassment and desperate need to speak to a total stranger about such personal things. She left with no indication of her intention to talk to The Doctor. I felt let down and disillusioned again at the lack of communication from another HP.

The next day the doctor who had shown me the scan told me that I would shortly be transferred to Rehab. This was six days after the stroke and I was elated. I expected to be home later that day.

The following morning as I was leaving the hospital, a speech therapist left me with a bundle of practice material and mentioned that I would see other therapists at Rehab.

As I waited for transport I thought about why my frustration had grown with every interaction with HPs. I realised that they had been ambivalent at best and oblivious at worst, to the anxiety that accompanies stroke. Perhaps their lack of empathy arose because they hadn't experienced stroke or over time they had become dulled to the plight of victims. After almost a week, the lack of recognition by most HPs of the devastating nature of losing one's language was evident. They had no concept of the trauma resulting from the inability to communicate and the impact of losing a lifetime of skills and independence.

On arrival at the Rehab Unit, I was taken to a ward and shown to a bed. My heart sank again. *But I don't want to stay here!* Two junior doctors examined me and treated me in a positive and respectful manner, but didn't mention the speech therapist, or going home. I didn't unpack my clothes as I kept watching for her, but she didn't come.

I busied myself that afternoon in a quiet area, listing some tasks to be done for my business, writing questions for Heather, and practising my self-initiated language exercises. I practised my handwriting and hand exercises, as I tried to recover the normal feeling in my hands—even trying to write with my left hand. I found a discarded newspaper and began reading, only to discover that reading paragraphs was very difficult. I noticed that one of the articles had been written by one of my journalist clients. But my brain couldn't scan smoothly across the words. It lurched across the phrases and I couldn't focus on individual lines or sentences. I was puzzled, but there had been no testing of this skill, and no mention of it as part of my brain injury. So I didn't ask anyone about it for fear of being seen to be less than capable, and kept longer in Rehab.

A senior doctor spoke to me briefly and I mentioned how I was using Bloom's Taxonomy to help myself. He remarked that he had some knowledge of this educational methodology. *Thank goodness someone knows what I'm trying to say!* He conducted a test of my walking. He said that if the speech therapist said it was OK, I could go home. *Is the speech therapist more powerful or knowledgeable than the doctors? Why is my level of language the issue? It isn't life threatening!* I stayed ever watchful for the speech therapist. By the end of the day there was no sign of her.

That evening I also spent some time working through the materials given to me by the hospital speech therapist at the last minute prior to transferring to Rehab. They contained some simple line drawings that were peculiar, to say the least. I assumed they were trick questions used by therapists to assess patients' comments or interpretations of what the figures were doing, or doing wrongly. The sheets showed a child running (drawn with same leg and hand forward instead of opposite leg and arm), a child cycling, an adult in bed being examined by a doctor (I laughed at the very '50s-style drawing and the doctor with her back to the patient while conducting observations), a person mowing the grass with an antiquated hand-pushed mower, and another raking up leaves in a garden. I noted the peculiarities and felt pleased with myself that at least I had identified them—a higher level of recognition, slowly heading back up the Bloom's Taxonomy ladder.

In this bundle of materials, there were also two pages of American-related general knowledge questions. I noticed that the publication date on the sheets was 1989. *Why isn't it a list of more recent Australian-based questions? What could be the benefit of knowing about the geography or history of America, while recovering from a stroke in Australia?*

That afternoon, I encountered the same lack of communication among the HPs in Rehab that had occurred in acute services:

"Have you had a bladder scan today?"

"What is a bladder scan? Is it an x-ray? Do I need to go somewhere? Is it like an ultrasound?"

"You need to have one every day."

"What is it? I haven't had one before. I thought I was here for my head not my bladder!"

"Just give me a sample as soon as you can."

(I obliged straight away).

"Do I need to go somewhere now for a scan?"

She grabbed the sample out of my hand and walked off without answering my question. She either didn't know how to explain it, or in keeping with the attitude that I had come to expect, clearly thought I had lost my intelligence and it wasn't worth giving me an explanation at all. No-one came to collect me to go anywhere.

> *Medical File Entry:*
> *'Asked patient to let nursing staff know when she goes to the toilet so we can do a PVBS, she was asked earlier but she was a bit confused re what we meant by bladder scan, explained procedure to patient again....'*

(The file comment was wrong. The HP showed disregard for using communication to suit the needs of the patient. There was no explanation at any time, nor was I asked earlier—only given a directive on this one occasion. The use of 'a bit confused' in a derogatory and inappropriate manner was a convenient term in my medical file by some HPs, even though I was clearly, and repeatedly, assessed as orientated to my surroundings. Did this incident need to be in the shift report at all? I certainly hadn't had a bladder scan each day—whatever it was. The evidence was in the lack of relevant data in my medical file).

I realised by 5.00pm it was too late to expect to see the speech therapist.

Next morning, I was surprised when approached by an occupational therapist. She asked me to accompany her to her office for an assessment. I thought she had made a mistake and told her I was waiting for the speech therapist. She assured me that her assessment was necessary. I followed her to an office to be seen as co-operative, though I was annoyed that it was a waste of time. *I don't want to miss the speech therapist!* She tested my skills using what looked like children's play money to calculate the payment required for purchase of a deep fryer pictured in an Aldi brochure. I asked her why she didn't use normal currency for her test. She shrugged her shoulders and insisted on me completing the test without explanation or discussion. I reluctantly complied, sceptical of the validity of this test.

I tried to explain to her that it was out of touch: I could buy what I needed online; pay using a card and have purchases delivered, if necessary. Why was there a pre-occupation with small purchases via cash—especially as I knew I wouldn't be able to drive—perhaps ever again? She didn't explain the relevance of the test or how it might validly indicate my skills or keep me safe.

Out of the Fog

Medical File Entry:
'Patient able to recognise Australian notes and coins.
(The play money didn't resemble Australian notes
and coins that I knew). Slow with sums and counting
out money amounts though managed with 90%
accuracy. (Errors were not out by large amounts).'

Did she ever consider that I might have been working slowly to make sure that I succeeded? That it was important for me to do things correctly for my self-esteem and confidence under the circumstances? Or was it easier to negatively label my response as 'slow'? Why did it matter that I was slow? At what speed would she say that I passed the test?

I found this assessment process patronising and insulting. I was incensed that she expected a person with a brain injury, to learn an unfamiliar currency quickly, and succeed in the test. Where was the validity in this test for real life, i.e. relevant tasks to an individual's needs? Was the test about using money? Or was it a more convenient way of testing and ticking the boxes for the HP—even if it was irrelevant to the patient?

She then tested me on dialling a phone. I couldn't remember Heather's number. *Why do I need to remember it? It's in the speed dial on my landline at home and in my mobile phone.* So she gave me a sheet of numbers to follow. I knew I couldn't follow the numbers written down in sequence. I couldn't even read them fluently. I had already discovered that for myself through my own efforts. So to look like I could do the test, I pressed eight numbers starting with the two for local calls, then quickly followed by some random others. She said that was OK. I did the same process for my own number (there was no explanation of why I needed to know how to dial my own number!). I had no idea which numbers I pressed. She couldn't possibly have seen or remembered what I dialled as she sat at an angle to the table on which I worked. In reality, even one wrong digit would render the number useless. So what did it test? How to press numbers on a phone? This didn't test my cognitive skills or sequencing of numbers that were relevant to my life. It wasn't done on equipment that resembled anything I had at home. I smiled to myself at the farcical nature of this assessment.

> *Medical File Entry:*
> *'Patient able to demonstrate use of a landline and ring her own home phone and also Heather's home phone. Couldn't remember this but could read some off my page and dial.'*

Later, when I read this entry in my file, I laughed out loud.

Unfortunately, on the basis of these questionable tests, with no knowledge of my telephone system, she had the power to make recommendations about my capacity to use my phone at home—and apparently be safe.

I hadn't used a telephone book in years with a list of regularly called numbers in speed dial. She didn't test my capacity to access the Internet to find numbers, which was my usual practice in my business. *She didn't test my capacity to dial 000 for an emergency. Wouldn't that be the logical number to ring if I found myself in difficulty? When would I ring my own phone? If anything, wouldn't she want to know how I could write my address accurately for identification when away from home, if I couldn't speak?* She didn't test that. No-one tested that.

During this session I showed her the sheets in my blue folder, which I had studied on the previous day, given to me by the hospital speech therapist. I asked her about my interpretation of their function. She looked surprised when I highlighted the absurdity of some of the drawings and questions. She remarked, "I've never noticed those things in the drawings before". *Has she used them for years, perhaps failing patients in tests who also saw them as absurd, but were unable to express or question what they saw in the pictures?*

I showed her my responses to the American general knowledge questions. I pointed out how many of them I had guessed in my written responses, because I didn't know anything about them. Against the question, 'What is the capital of Georgia?" I wrote, 'I don't know but it makes damned good jazz.' We laughed about my comment.

I assured her that as soon as I arrived home I would purchase a VitalCall service for emergencies. Having passed the assessment with her assurance that I would be OK to go home, I returned downstairs to wait for the speech therapist.

I asked a nurse again when the therapist might come. She said, "I don't know. You'll have to wait". I had a sense of déjà vu!

Shortly after, the occupational therapist passed me again in the corridor.

> "Tomorrow (Friday) or Monday we'll take you shopping and when you go home, we'll assess your skills in being safe".
> "I haven't given you my consent to take me shopping. I have no clothes here aside from nightwear, so I can't go shopping anyway. You will not set foot on my property, much of which is set up for my business. How can you possibly test and make recommendations on my safety in that environment when you know nothing about it?"

By this stage I was very angry and exasperated at her assumption that showed disregard for my rights to choose whether or not to participate in this exercise, no regard for my privacy, and no knowledge of what she was assessing. Even with my difficulty in thinking logically, I could see how illogical it was for her to assess me at home. She knew nothing about how my home and business had been closely integrated over almost 30 years. What right did she have to make any judgments about my safety in this environment, or how it should operate?

Yet she had an unfettered, legal power to make judgments and record them in my medical file, as permanent entries. I was determined that I would never let that happen.

As the time dragged on in the afternoon, I became frustrated at my futile wait for the speech therapist. By 4.00pm, I knew she wouldn't come that day.

Then John, Winsome and Sandy from choir arrived with Bernard, and to my relief suggested we go for coffee away from Rehab. I felt grateful that my friends would at least give me some respite and treat me positively.

As we returned, an angry nurse confronted me in the corridor, blocking my path. She made loud and unreasonable demands, causing a very embarrassing scene in front of my visitors. To my horror, the directive that Heather had arranged with the hospital during the previous week to allay my fear for my safety, had been ignored. I rejected her demands and summoned all of my strength to strongly refuse her directive: verbally and with gestures. It was unmistakeable what I meant.

Shortly after, when my visitors had left, the nurse confronted me again in the television room. She persisted in her demands and stood over me in a threatening manner. I was exhausted, stressed and very afraid for my safety. She left the room. As it was around 5.00pm and becoming dark, I knew that I couldn't leave on my own at night, so I resolved to leave the following morning. After three days in Rehab, I no longer cared that I hadn't spoken to the speech therapist.

I sat quietly in the corner of the room behind a stored bed screen where I felt safe. I had no contact with anyone for almost nine hours, until well after midnight when *The Late Show* with David Letterman came on the television. Suddenly, a nurse walked into the room and flicked on the light. In confronting me, she indicated her dissatisfaction. I felt like a child being chastised for being in the television room and not in bed. I was shocked at her manner.

My medical file did not report these events fully. There was no record of the nurse's belligerent and belittling behaviour, and that no-one had attempted to assure me of my safety at any time, even though they knew I was afraid. The brief entry that *was* entered in my file was erroneous by omission of the details of the events that had transpired.

The following morning, I woke early and made sure that all of my belongings were packed and ready. At around 7.30am I approached a senior nurse to tell her of my intention to leave.

I spoke slowly and carefully so that she could make no mistake about my reasons. She urged me to stay, but when I insisted, she said, "I'll arrange a prescription from the doctor to take with you". (This was surprising, as I hadn't been given medication in Rehab, assuming the medical staff had stopped it.) When reading my file later, I found that the medication had been missed for two days. On the third day it was *entered* as administered probably by someone who realised that the medication had not been given—but it was not given to me. No HPs spoke to me or approached me for any purpose after I stated that I was leaving; not even for a bladder scan! Apparently, because I had decided to self-discharge, clearly I was not entitled to any care.

> *Medical File Entry:*
> *'Met with Mrs Henderson today as she was pacing the*
> *corridors and wanting to go home.'*

Given the events of the previous night, this comment showed disregard for the fear that had led to me hiding for more than eight hours in the television room. It was a value judgment and an insensitive comment from another HP in a leadership position. If it was intended that I would be discharged that day, why didn't she tell me when I spoke to her? Instead she tried to persuade me to stay. At no time did she mention leaving, because I still hadn't been seen by the speech therapist on whose assessment, apparently, I would stay or be discharged on whatever day she felt was appropriate.

The senior nurse's remark of 'pacing the corridors while waiting for the prescription' referred to me walking out to the foyer of the building or standing in the doorway of my room—across from the nurses' station—so I could be seen, as a silent reminder that I was waiting for the prescription. Several times, I walked up to the television room and sat in the doorway out of the way of the busy ward, but able to observe the corridor at the front of the nurses' station. At one stage, I saw the senior nurse leave, then some time later return to her desk. But she didn't come near me to give me a prescription, so again I waited.

The speech therapist arrived shortly after 10.00am. After she introduced herself, I stated slowly and clearly:

> "You're too late, I'm going home. There will be no assessment, no treatment and nothing more from this place. But as you will not be aware of what has happened to me here, I'll explain to you why I am leaving now".

After my explanation she left to complete her report.

Medical File Entry:
'Initially unco-operative, but agreeable to conversation—no assessment.'

(After this entry, there follows a lengthy assessment of my language despite my refused consent. In what circumstances does the patient ever have any power or rights in this environment? Why was asserting my rights seen as 'unco-operative'? Where was respect for my decision to refuse consent for further assessment? The assessment of my language was not life-threatening, and my refusal should have been accepted, not criticised).

A social worker arrived at 11.00am and introduced herself. I said:

> "You're too late. I am going home. I don't want any more services. But it's not your fault, so I will explain why."

She listened to my explanation and was genuinely concerned, but I reiterated my refusal for further assistance. She respected my decision. She did not conduct or write a social work assessment report, aside from a brief entry, indicating my decision to have no further assessment or assistance.

At 11.25am, after four hours of waiting for the prescription, I approached a group of three nurses standing at the nurses' station. They saw but didn't acknowledge me. While almost falling over each other like a comedy sketch from 'Fawlty Towers', they immediately turned away and began foraging together in a cupboard. So I approached the senior nurse that I had spoken to earlier:

> "If the prescription isn't here in five minutes, I'll leave without it."
> "I'll check if it's here."

She turned the page on an open file in front of her, picked up the prescription and handed it to me. Snatching it out of her hand I turned and walked back to gather my belongings. I was very angry.

I carried my bags unassisted to the foyer placing my blue folder on top. I asked the receptionist to call for a taxi and she quickly ran out of the room. When she returned shortly afterwards, presumably with permission to grant my request, she called the taxi.

I had to be home by 12.00md. I knew that Barb, a long time friend and neighbour, had been looking after my home. I knew that she would leave at that time to care for an elderly family member. After that, I would have no access to my premises, which had been securely locked during my absence. *How will I pay for the taxi if I can't get inside?*

With now only 25 minutes to get home (it's a 30-minute journey in traffic), I was very concerned that I wouldn't make it in time.

While I waited in the foyer near the front door, the occupational therapist that I had spoken to the previous day walked up to me and briskly handed me the application for the VitalCall Service. I immediately noticed her angry facial expression, in complete contrast to the laughter we had shared over my comment about Georgia. Now she looked stone-faced with no eye contact. Noticing her body language, I turned to her:

"Please don't be angry with me. This is my decision to leave, it's nothing to do with you."

"You have some materials that belong to the Hospital that you can't have."

"What do I have? I only have my own belongings!"

"They're in that folder."

I quickly opened the blue folder, and on top were the sheets we had laughed about the previous day.

In a spiteful action, with no further comment, she snatched the sheets out of the folder and quickly walked away to the steps leading to her office. I was shocked and dismayed. I couldn't understand why she had removed material given to me by another HP, which was intended to help me. I resolved to follow up this incident later.

The taxi pulled up in front of me at that moment, and I quickly loaded my belongings into the boot. The senior nurse stood in the doorway of the foyer watching me but didn't speak. The social worker came up to me and I thanked her for her concern, but I refused her offer for money to pay the taxi. I knew that I could use a card to pay for the fare at home.

As I left the hospital, urging the taxi driver that I was in a hurry, I had a sense of great relief—like passing over a border to safety and freedom.

Chapter Three

Solo

I was very pleased to see Barb as I arrived home, a few minutes before midday. She was shocked but not surprised to see me. Heather and Annette arrived shortly after, having already travelled to the hospital, and found that I had left for home. I offered them coffee, taking far too long during its preparation because I needed reminding of their preferences several times. While we chatted, I could hardly contain my sense of freedom. I tried to join in the conversation but even in my own environment, I became frustrated at my stumbling words.

I was very grateful that my treasured friends stayed with me until they felt I was settled enough to be on my own. As they left to get on with their respective days, they made sure that I had an appointment with my local GP, and communication systems were in place with email, mobile phone and Skype. I sensed that they were guarded in their happiness at my escape, so I assured them as confidently as I could, that I would be OK on my own.

But in my heart I was very frightened. I had no idea what would happen next: *Will I suffer another stroke alone? How can I recover my language—with access to the health service as the only known resource now eliminated? Will I play the piano again? What will happen to my business if I don't recover my language?* But come what may— I resolved I would not go back to the hospital!

Barb called in again during that afternoon, "Just passing", she said. I was very grateful for her concern and welcomed her company for a chat.

Alone after she left, I felt a heightened fear about the way ahead as I began to think about the previous nine days. I thought about what had led to this situation. More importantly: what can I do to fix it? With little ability to think clearly, and with a sense of trepidation, I had few answers.

By early evening, I was fatigued in re-orientating myself to my home and afraid to do much of anything. The elation of my return home was diminished to some degree by my realisation of the demands of coping alone with the effects of the stroke. I wanted to know the true extent of my loss of communication skills. *What does it really mean for my future and my business?* Having been given no hope by the HPs, I was very fearful of what I might discover if I tried to do even simple tasks. At that time, I believed I was incapable of regaining the independence I had previously enjoyed.

I accepted that the stroke had occurred, but I felt angry that in my vulnerable state my self-confidence had been shattered, with no negotiation, by a health service that had continually disregarded my rights, intuition and what I knew was best for me. This increased my fear about my potential loss of independence if I couldn't cope at home alone. I sought the comfort of sleep. As my brain had learned to operate on short naps for so long, I woke frequently and spent a night of restless sleep.

When I woke the following morning, I was faced with the stark reality of the severity of my brain injury and my cognitive and physical failures. I desperately wanted to rebuild my life as quickly as possible, so I was already frightened and anxious. I didn't know where to start.

I began tentatively with some simple tasks. I thoroughly enjoyed using my own shower and dressing in comfortable clothes again. I thought carefully through each small task to make sure I did it correctly. As I put on some casual shoes I congratulated myself on tying my shoelaces, even with my slow-moving fingers. I saw this complex task as a real achievement. It became one of the first entries in my diary later that day. I also felt elated that I could make toast and tea. I was happy that at least I could make simple food to feed myself.

Barb called in early, as she did on many occasions during the ups and downs of the next few days and weeks. She was cheerful and compassionate so I was always comforted by her visits. She allowed me to fail my words without judgment, and I was very grateful for her patience.

That morning, I sent my first post-stroke email. I wasn't sure if I could complete this task, so I worked slowly and deliberately to send a simple message.

> *Email Message to Heather:*
> *I'm slow but okay. I will locate on the net about a blood pressure machine so I can watch it daily after my appointment at doctor. Which one?*

This message took a long time to write. It indicated how my brain was lurching from one idea to the next, searching for the right pathway. I became frustrated while writing these few words, as I couldn't sort them out to be more coherent. They were longer sentences than I had written in my diary while in hospital.

I cautiously tried to read a few messages that had arrived from clients while I had been in hospital. I was shocked that I couldn't read them fluently and quickly. My eyes refused to flow across the text, my brain faltered by missing many words and the messages were unintelligible. I worried that I couldn't work again. I couldn't understand how I was ever going to recover my reading skills that were such an essential part of my business. After a few minutes of trying, I left the computer. I was afraid of failure in trying to send replies to let my clients know that I was home and functioning again. In reality, I felt far from functioning normally.

During my second attempt at reading emails several hours later, I looked at some that Heather and Annette had sent to clients each day while I was in hospital. I found myself reading a few words, then having to re-read the same phrase many times. I couldn't understand or remember what it said or link the words in a sentence. However, as I very slowly began to recognise the same informative messages to multiple clients, their words began to fall into place. Gradually, some messages from new clients started to make some sense. For others, such as clients with previous and ongoing messages, it was impossible to remember the links to immediately understand their context.

At that early stage, I realised that I would have to re-read, research and re-write information many times before I could send even a simple but coherent reply to clients. But a fleeting glimpse of optimism arose, when my scrambled brain could sometimes find its pathway. I realised that if I read the same message repeatedly, correctly and slowly, I could understand bits and pieces of their messages. But at that stage, it was not enough to give me real confidence.

Tiring quickly, I frantically tried to think through a way of getting around this problem to minimise the impact on my business. Trying to cope with the rising apprehension that surged through my mind, I was overwhelmed with the thought of struggling with even the simplest office procedures. Again I experienced many brick walls and black holes in trying to recognise and follow threads of information, while attempting desperately with what seemed to be simple emails. Complex or lengthy messages were completely beyond my comprehension.

Self-doubt rose and spilled over in my thoughts, preventing me thinking of a way around these difficulties. *Perhaps I can't do it after all. Were the HPs right? Maybe I have lost my intelligence.* I was despondent and frustrated that I couldn't analyse and think through anything, with my concentration lasting for only a few seconds. My effort seemed futile. I felt miserable and unable to think rationally about any positives in my future.

Abandoning the computer again, I forced myself to ask, *what skills do I still have?* By trying to think more calmly, I reminded myself that I had written in short phrases while in hospital. This had reduced the errors in my diary and helped me in writing down so much about my experience.

So, again I focused on using trigger words and phrases. If I could transcribe them correctly into simple sentences, perhaps this may hide my fractured language, and be a tool to renew and maintain my contact with my clients. My hope grew at the possibility of this strategy. I hypothesised that if I took my time with composing a list of simple sentences stored in a word processing file, I could construct, copy and paste coherent messages into the email replies. I could read and alter them as necessary, using various online dictionaries, a thesaurus, spelling and grammar checker tools,

Just as quickly, my self-doubt emerged again; given the number of emails I received in each workday. It seemed impossible and overwhelmingly time-consuming. *How long and consistently can I work in this way given my difficulty in concentration and linking information? How productive will it be, given the volume of work each day? Is it totally unrealistic?* I became exhausted with my speeding thoughts, in thinking about the logistics of this plan. There seemed to be no pathway to success.

This was an unfamiliar situation that I now found myself in—that I didn't know how to manage and overcome a challenge. Throughout my adult life, and in running a business, I had grasped challenges with both hands. I had always found that, 'there is always an alternative' in finding a solution to problems. Now, my previous confidence had deserted me in putting any plan into action. It was replaced with a fear of failure. In my rising anxiety and diminished cognitive ability, I couldn't think through even simple solutions or remember anything that might have been logical about the idea. The more I tried to gain control of my thinking, the more I failed.

An hour's sleep helped me to forget my frustration for a short time. I awoke and started reading the emails again. By that evening, I had read a long list of emails aloud, very slowly, but in a very fragmented way. I used the mouse to highlight the words a few at a time, forcing myself to pronounce them correctly to make sense of the message. It was tedious and exhausting. However, by the time I finished late that night, I had understood several short messages and felt that I had achieved something: *But is it sustainable? Is it useful? I haven't responded to any. Can I write coherently beyond a few words at a time?*

I tossed and turned through another restless night, often wide-awake for long periods, and trying to make sense of my life now. In the darkness, I thought about why the events of the past nine days had happened, and what might happen in the future.

My mind travelled through many thoughts. I reminded myself that I was overweight. Through the years I had given only cursory attention to occasional warnings in the media that being overweight could lead to health problems such as stroke. While my weight had increased during middle age, I hadn't seen it as a real problem. Perhaps I was in denial. But in the previous 12 months, I knew that my weight had quickly and significantly increased. In the back of my mind it was always going to be something to be dealt with during retirement.

Over the years, I had learned that in small business there was little time to be ill. I hadn't experienced anything more than the occasional cold, and there had been no obvious need to visit my GP for many years.

But why had the stroke happened now, with no recognisable symptoms of my dangerous level of hypertension? What had changed? In the solitude and stillness of the winter night, it wasn't difficult to see the reasons, even with an injured brain.

During the preceding twelve months, my business had grown more quickly than usual. I integrated the additional work into my role rather than employing more staff. I knew my workload had become horrendous and unsustainable. But it became such a burden, that ironically, I couldn't see a way to take time out to train someone else. It was an increasingly negative cycle. Something had to give.

In the early months of that year, as I had become accustomed to having only a few hours sleep at night, it seemed that I could reduce my sleep even further. I trained myself to become adept at taking short naps when needed, and I gradually began to work longer hours without normal sleep. I learned to regularly work through two or three days with several short naps being my only rest. Initially, this enabled me to keep up with my rapidly increasing workload, fulfil my responsibilities to the two choirs with rehearsals and frequent gigs (more than 60 that year), care for my elderly dogs, and do the myriad of ordinary things that are part of everyday life.

But almost everything I did was sedentary: working at the computer for long hours editing and writing many types of business documents, completing all the administration for the business, consulting with clients on their careers, training them in interview skills, driving long distances to interviewing and consulting jobs, and playing the piano for the choirs at rehearsals and gigs each week.

My frantic schedule left me no time for exercise. I had never particularly enjoyed exercise through my adult life anyway—mostly because it seemed too strenuous while being overweight. Another irony! With my busy workload, it was something that could be conveniently ignored.

As the months wore on, I had become aware that I was eating more, gaining weight and coping less. Multiple cups of coffee (often up to 10 in a day) and meals several times in the day or the night gave me the energy to keep working. Sometimes I felt very agitated. On three separate but very busy days over several weeks in the months prior to the stroke, I had felt chest palpitations. On each of these occasions, a short nap enabled me to go back to work with little lost time. These episodes were probably a warning of my increasing hypertension. I had ignored them as irritations.

I had often felt tired, was not enjoying my job as I had done over the preceding years, and wondered at times whether I should consider retirement. So I had resolved to work through the following few months and call it quits. But it wasn't what I *wanted* to do, as I had always loved my work and my business. Many times, I had experienced the exhilarating sense of achievement that comes from building your own successful business, and doing a job that you really enjoy!

Now, with my impaired ability to think logically and no idea how to recover from the stroke, it seemed that to fix the catastrophic situation I found myself in, I had to at least do something about my weight. *Surely that will help. OK, I know the solution to that problem. Tomorrow, I'll start exercising.* Sleep came.

The next morning, I woke excitedly knowing that Annette was calling in for coffee. True to my resolution overnight, I began the day with a walk. I was back in 20 minutes, afraid to go far from home. But at least I had made a start.

I welcomed Annette a few hours later. Then, as we chatted, she casually asked:

"Have you tried to play the piano?"
"No."
"Well, why don't we give it a try?"

I felt nervous. I felt sick. Being an optimist, she had challenged me. Not wanting to disappoint her and knowing that she wouldn't judge me if I failed, deep down I needed to know. A wave of apprehension came over me—I was being confronted with another 'test'—another potential failure. Here was the looming answer to my repeated question in hospital and the potentially devastating realisation of my loss. *But what if I can't play at all? What if I can't read the music?*

I also knew, that even if I was afraid, I had to maintain the impression that I was determined and capable, which had justified my leaving hospital. But more than anything, I wanted to keep her faith in me. In my heart, I was desperate to return to the choirs and the wonderful friends who had supported me before and since the stroke. Their good wishes, emails, visits and the unconditional friendships I had made over many years, were very special to me in my fragile state. But until this moment, no-one had confronted me with 'the question'.

I had played piano since childhood. As an adult, I had played professionally for almost 15 years in the entertainment industry. I had many wonderful experiences participating in many different forms of music as a solo artist, an accompanist for many singers, and a performer in bands. My long career in music had included classical, musical theatre, cabaret, opera, jazz, blues, and rock. Having retired from the demands of the entertainment industry, I had found myself, almost by accident, accompanying two fabulous community choirs, for fun. I had come to love them, feeling more welcomed by these groups than any others in my life. The thought was devastating that I may have lost my skills to play and miss the positive, fun and social relationships that we enjoyed each week. It was more than I could contemplate.

I felt sad that I might not be able to work with William anymore. We had enjoyed such good times together as we wound our way through the mysteries and joys of music at rehearsals each week. I had so much to teach him and he had such a thirst for knowledge. I had admired his emerging talent in arranging songs and his beautiful touch on the piano. I had been so proud to be a part of his life at this time in his musical career.

But in hospital, the HPs repeatedly dismissed my question, "Will I play piano again?" Their avoidance of any discussion of the possibility had intensified my fear. They had given me no hope that I could, and so I assumed that I had lost these skills completely as a result of the stroke.

This had also been reinforced by accident on one occasion in hospital. Annette had taken me to a café for coffee, where there was a piano being played by someone who looked like an accomplished pianist. Given my vast knowledge of music, I wondered why it was unrecognisable. Seeing my look of dismay, Annette said, "It's just someone playing around". I knew it was worse than that—I had lost part of my soul.

51

Now, with Annette quietly raising the challenge I felt very afraid of failure if I tried to play. I had vivid recollection of losing my proficiency in reading music falling away by the second at the time of the stroke.

During the first day at home, I had walked past the piano many times. But I couldn't bring myself to look at it or even to sit down at the keyboard. My beloved music books had remained untouched.

Annette waited patiently for my response. I picked up one of the choir books and placed it on the music stand. I opened the volume at a random page. It was 'Morning Has Broken' a favourite for the choir and me. (I recorded it as 'Morning Glory' in my diary entry later that day). I looked at the music and desperately wanted to play it! So I sat at the piano, trying to summon my strength to overcome my anxiety. I took a deep breath. I started playing hesitantly, slowly and softly. I felt like a beginner. My hands and fingers still felt swollen, stiff and slow to move. But as my brain started to falteringly read the familiar music, its beautiful melody began to flow. I could feel myself starting to relax and my anxiety turning to excitement. Annette began to sing. I played the first verse, stumbling occasionally, my eyes lurching through the chords and the music. I realised with extraordinary relief that my skills were still there, at least to some degree.

I looked at Annette to find her singing through her tears. Through my own tears I continued to play to the end. We rejoiced that I could play and that my fears were apparently unfounded. I scarcely allowed myself to believe that I could play for the choirs again.

It was impossible for me to explain how I felt that day—the exhilaration and excitement—for the first time since the stroke. I dared to believe that there was some hope for regaining my skills in something that was very personal and important to me. For a short while, my joy was also mixed with anger. This could have been discovered in hospital and reduced my anxiety significantly, if the HPs had shown flexibility or creativity in their assessments.

The next day, I woke early and went for a walk. This time it was half an hour before I returned home. It gave me 'thinking time' as I enjoyed the freshness of the early winter morning. I thought about how good it felt, that on the previous day I had loosened the shackles of frustration in one way, by taking a big leap back into life in another. I congratulated myself on my success. I knew that I had to keep trying to crawl out of the fog to freedom again, across all areas of my life. I promised myself that no matter how difficult or frustrating it was going to be, I had to try. I needed to regain control, confidence and independence.

So an hour later, 13 days after the stroke, and three days after leaving hospital, I went back to work. It seemed logical that I could achieve optimal recovery by going back to work to whatever level was feasible in my own familiar environment, in the same way as injured workers are encouraged to return to work as quickly as possible.

I knew that if I convinced myself—and believed—that I could recover, I would embark on this task in a positive way. I needed to counter the gloomy outlook that had characterised the approach used by the HPs.

But where to start? What resources do I have? It occurred to me that I could practise regaining my skills in reading, comprehension, writing and speaking by searching, exploring, downloading and reading information on stroke recovery from the Internet. This would be more useful than spending hours doing meaningless, childlike exercises with no real function, plan, direction or foreseeable outcome.

With millions of online articles and websites on stroke recovery and loss of language, can I search through this mountain of information to find what is useful for me? Can I understand it? Can I put it into practice with no safety net from the health system?

I began to look through the Cochrane Collaboration Library for clinical abstracts and readable articles. To focus my brain and my eyes, I moved the mouse a few words at a time. I worked for only a few minutes before taking a break. I read aloud, practising and repeating words and phrases. It was very slow work.

I set a target of finding and printing three useful articles for each short reading session. By lunchtime I had assembled a pile of articles and bookmarked some less heavy websites. While I hadn't read anything thoroughly by this stage, I felt that I was at least doing something productive to help myself.

During that afternoon, I tentatively checked a few client emails that had arrived that day. I worked very slowly. I found that by writing a very short response, leaving it for a while, and then reading again and adjusting it several times before sending, I could make it readable—and mostly correct (as I found when I re-read them many weeks later). I finished the day with a sense of achievement that I had taken the first steps in a long road of recovery.

The next day I began with a short walk. Then Barb drove me to visit Ken, my GP. He was startled when I informed him that I had discharged myself from hospital after a stroke. I hadn't visited him for many years so he had few references to my medical history on file. Given my fractured language, I explained what I could. Although he didn't show or express any judgment of my actions, I felt it was important to sound like I was lucid. It was exhausting trying to speak clearly about some of the events that had occurred in hospital. He looked dismayed when I related the episode with the occupational therapist removing my practice materials from my belongings as I left the hospital. He had no answers.

While trying to explain what had happened, I failed miserably with my words, frequently stumbling and faltering. My anxiety was high and I felt traumatised by the experience. As the memories were very raw, I fought back tears.

With no Discharge Summary from the hospital immediately available, Ken systematically began the process of building up a profile of my current health status by arranging some routine tests. He suggested twice-weekly appointments.

After returning home, I began reading some of the material that I had printed from the Internet about stroke recovery. From the first article I read slowly, word-by-word, and sentence-by-sentence. I frequently had to re-read the information, as much of it was complex, technical and incomprehensible to my injured brain. I began to realise the mammoth task ahead. I could work for only for a few minutes, reading the words aloud several times, writing down a few key words and then proceeding with the next few sentences. My intention was to gradually build my own library of reference material and keep practising my language. I failed miserably.

After half an hour of this gruelling process, with few coherent notes written, I was exhausted and despondent. I couldn't remember anything I had read, even after checking my scratchy notes.

I took a break and tried to watch television, but the presenters seemed to be speaking too quickly. I had to sit very close to the screen in order to understand what they were saying. I managed to understand a few words when they were facing the camera, but not as voice-overs. *Why can't I understand them?* The sound amplified through the speakers sounded like they were speaking in a foreign language. I turned up the television volume, but the sound became more distorted and unintelligible. I left the television and went back to work.

I had no choice but to push myself. I tried editing a business profile partially completed for a client. I learned that by enlarging the text, sliding the mouse over a few words at a time and concentrating as hard as possible, I could read reasonably fluently. I could follow phrases better because the white space next to or around the blue highlighted area helped in focusing my eyes.

I persevered to finally reach the end of a sentence by reading aloud, often stumbling with even simple words, re-reading and trying to say a phrase aloud with rhythm. I used the punctuation where it occurred, then highlighted and added in the next phrase. When I failed in saying a complex word, I took a deep breath, then broke the word down into one or more separate syllables, layered the rhythm and voice intonation onto the syllables and practised it until I could say it fluently. This seemed to work, because after a while I had made sense of some small bits of the material I was reading. This became my strategy in reading anything from the computer. It was a tedious process, but I wanted to re-acquaint my brain with the sound of the words, the rhythm of language, and recover my skills in comprehension as quickly as possible.

Over the next few days I tried this simple technique when reading emails from clients. As they were often only a few words or lines, I could read, follow the message and reply to them more confidently. This worked especially if I used a simple reply.

I frequently gave myself a little summary or word test at the end of paragraphs of research abstracts, just to check that I was making progress. I talked myself through the test—sometimes succeeding, sometimes failing miserably. The successes became the motivating force based on my belief that if I could succeed with re-learning one word, I could re-learn a thousand.

I left the computer for quick breaks. I often walked around the garden, recalling any phrases or key words I could remember from articles that I had read a few minutes earlier or from email messages. I saw each waking moment as a 'teachable moment'. My productivity began to increase although I often tired quickly. However, I knew I was making some tiny gains. So I persevered.

I read widely, slowly and deliberately, initially seeking Australian research. As my comprehension began to improve even slightly, there seemed to be little that was useful or innovative beyond the approach that had been used by the HPs in hospital. *Where is the creativity? Where is the motivating spirit to give people hope?* By the time I read several times, 'If the skills have not been regained within 12 months, they probably won't be regained', and, 'After 1–2 years they often reach a plateau', my hope that I could fully recover was starting to falter. The material seemed to be unnecessarily pessimistic. *How hard will I have to work to regain my skills in 12 months in light of this gloomy picture?* The mountain ahead of me seemed to be too high with impossible barriers. But in other moments, I refused to believe that I couldn't achieve more than the research suggested. I refused to be bound by it. I grasped onto these moments as a lifeline to motivate me to look for more positive strategies.

During the second week at home, Bernard, my IT Consultant and his wife Elizabeth emailed me that they would call in for coffee. Over the years I had always enjoyed their visits and I always made a delicious morning tea because of the long trip to my office from his business.

When he visited me in hospital, Bernard gave me a beautiful recipe book to remind me that he expected some of the lovely treats when next time he visited my business. Now, I looked at the book and found it almost impossible to follow. I had no idea if I could cook anything more complicated than toast, or open a can of baked beans. For the previous few days, very simple food had been sufficient.

Although I had managed to make coffee for other visitors, for Bernard and Elizabeth I wanted it to appear like 'business as usual' and make my usual scrumptious morning tea. I decided to make something simple and leave the new book for another time. I pulled out my folder of favourite recipes and quickly looked for ANZAC cookies. *What could be simpler than that?* I decided to at least give it a go, though I felt far from confident.

By 7.30am I started cooking for their 10.30am visit. I had made these cookies hundreds of times over the years, but now I had no confidence in completing the task without the recipe. After gathering the ingredients, I read and checked the quantity for each item in the recipe many times, to make sure I had the right ingredient and the right amount. For a simple list, it was a frustratingly slow process checking the weight of items several times, not trusting myself, then measuring again and checking again. Before mixing, I had to read every word in the recipe's method multiple times and try to follow each phrase to do things in the right order. Although the recipe was simple to read, I experienced the same difficulty as reading the stroke recovery articles—my eyes couldn't smoothly glide over the page. When my brain couldn't link the words, often a simple step didn't make sense.

It took well over an hour to prepare the cookies ready for baking—a job that pre-stroke would have taken me just a few minutes. Although there had been some improvement, my hands were still feeling swollen and stiff. To roll the spoonfuls of mixture between my hands was very difficult, as I couldn't bend my fingers easily. At last I managed to set out the cookies on the tray and I set the stove timer. I stood in the kitchen doing very little but watching the timer in case I missed the sound of the bell. The aroma was very comforting and the cookies looked good. They were the best ANZACs I had ever tasted, and were enjoyed with good friends. It was a simple achievement, but it had profound implications in the bigger picture of striving to reclaim the independence and control over my life that I had previously enjoyed—one step at a time.

Later that day, I started working on a report on the interviews held on the day of the stroke. But transferring complex notes taken in the interview into comprehensive and coherent sentences after three weeks, with an injured brain, seemed almost impossible. My memory of the interview was sketchy and my notes were largely unintelligible due to my loss of comprehension.

For a short while, my confidence disappeared in my ability to complete the report to the standard expected by my client. *What should I do? Should I contact the client and let them know that I can't do the job? Have I really given it a go? Or given up without really trying?*

I reminded myself then, and on many subsequent occasions, that my personal effort was the best tool that I could use to steer the pathway to my former level of skills. Taking responsibility for my own recovery meant that I wasn't at the mercy of people who were less committed to my needs, and who preferred to cast a dark shadow of hopelessness than look for a new pathway. *If I*

am to resume working fully in my business, then I have to find a way
around the problem! The alternative is not an alternative at all. I
went back to my hand-written notes and began reading slowly
at the first line, a few words at a time. I used a highlighter pen
to mark words or phrases that I had taken down quickly that
were more difficult to understand. I resolved to return to them
later. As I slowly began to decipher my notes, I set up the report
word-by-word.

By that night I had compiled the first of many sections to be
completed. The next day I emailed Shvon, my client's Executive
Officer to let her know that the report was underway. She was very
understanding. Her mother had lost her language with a stroke, so
she was fully aware of my difficulties when I contacted her. I was
grateful for her support and positive approach. I assured her that I
would complete the report as quickly as I could.

This was the first major job I attempted for my clients. I couldn't
set myself a target for completion because I had no real sense of when
I could finish it. But with some progress I knew that I had to keep
going and complete the job. Where I had normally taken a few hours
to produce similar reports, it took me almost six days of reading, re-
reading, changing text and forcing myself to read the report many
times to have it ready to send to Shvon.

It had been far from smooth sailing. Although I disciplined
myself to stay focused to build my self-confidence, sometimes I
couldn't read or write another word. On many occasions my brain
couldn't cope with the demand, and gave up. But I didn't take any
more than brief respite, before quickly resuming my schedule. As I
processed the email to send the completed report to Shvon, I dared
to have a sense of achievement in beginning to claw my way back
to normality.

During the ensuing days, I pushed myself as much as I could to
take more tiny steps towards recovery. I felt I was working against the
clock to regain my skills as quickly as possible before the '12-month
limit'. I couldn't imagine what it would be like to only have partially

regained my skills after only a year and suddenly being seen to have reached the finishing post. *What will happen then? Will I begin to deteriorate and lose my skills anyway?*

By the afternoons I could sometimes concentrate only for a few minutes. I found that I had to work in silence and discipline myself to keep working. I had become accustomed to listening to soft background music while working but now it was distracting. I took more frequent and longer breaks in the late afternoon and evening, then always returned to my targets and did a little more. My determination occasionally wavered but my self-confidence began to grow with the tiniest success—reading for one more minute than the last time without being distracted or giving up. Sometimes, I could lengthen this to around five more minutes in order to keep going, rather than give in to a sense of failure. Although it was slow, I reminded myself: each step was a success!

I continued to look for research in my desperate search to find ways to treat my injured brain. I began reading European and American research and useful websites. Without too much effort, I found that there was a more positive outlook in overseas articles than I had read in Australian research. It seemed logical, positive and much more hopeful. It was often more readable. I decided that was the best approach for me.

A recurrent theme in this research was that support for stroke recovery should be 'immediate and intensive.' By accident, out of desperation, I had begun that process for myself in hospital 12 hours after the stroke when Heather gave me the writing pad. I had engaged immediately in my own recovery and maintained continual practice each day, working intuitively and intensively with my visitors and when alone. This had not been the approach taken or welcomed by the HPs. Now, without the obstacles of the hospital, I had intuitively and significantly increased the intensity through my own efforts at home.

I spent a long time trying to make sense of the information, to give me some clue of what to do from a different perspective.

In addition to research, which was sometimes beyond me in my loss of comprehension skills (or sheer tiredness), I found extracts from books written by people who had experienced stroke, or were family members, some HPs (including several who had suffered stroke themselves), and carers. There were two recurring ideas: 1. That recovering skills after stroke was best done in the person's own environment, where possible. 2. Many people had experienced pessimism and negative experiences in the hospital environment. From this, I knew that to be in control of my own destiny was in itself more likely to yield positive outcomes.

I began to look around my limited world, and drew on anything that I could easily access as tools.

Through frequent contact with Heather and Annette I could let out my frustrations, talk through my 'down days'—without fear of rejection, derision or judgment—and celebrated when I was elated over even a small success. If I was tired or frustrated with my progress, email and Skype were invaluable for communication when my brain couldn't keep up with a conversation on the phone. At no time were they pessimistic, nor did they caution me from implementing the steady but intensive schedule I had set for myself. They supported me at every step in making my own decisions about my recovery. This boosted my motivation to keep trying when I felt the job was too hard.

I was grateful for my many other friends whose visits provided opportunities to talk, even in a fractured way, engaging in conversation and banter on any topic. I encouraged them to challenge my opinions on anything. In this way I had to think about and analyse ideas, compare and substantiate my arguments, and speak as coherently as I could. One afternoon over coffee, I debated the merits of some aspects of health services with Cynthia and Kay, two friends from choir. I *think* I won….

Barb showed infinite patience in driving me to the local medical centre and local pathology services. Ken had ordered a barrage of tests and she helped me communicate with the receptionists.

She became my interpreter. They seemed to have such soft voices and rapid speech. In the noisy waiting areas I frequently had to ask them to repeat their questions several times. I felt frustrated and embarrassed when I couldn't find the words to respond, and I quickly forgot what they had asked me. Barb often had to carefully explain to me what was needed.

The difficulty of following other people's conversations began to be even more obvious in my everyday activities. When the alarm woke me in the morning, I couldn't understand why the radio station that I regularly listened to seemed to be unfamiliar, and the radio presenter was hard to follow. I realised that I had experienced this problem the day after returning home from hospital, when I couldn't understand the television voice-overs. I had put it down to tiredness.

I noticed that even if I watched the clock timer tick over the hour, I often missed the ABC Radio news jingle. My brain heard only occasional familiar words. *What does this mean? Is my hearing affected by the stroke?* The sound of the newsreader's voice was muffled and difficult to understand—like someone speaking too fast and in a different language. At that stage, I had no idea that my brain could not keep up with the sound without visual cues from the speaker's face.

On my next visit to Ken I talked to him about my 'hearing difficulty'. He referred me for a hearing test. The results of the test showed that my hearing was normal for my age. He explained that the problem was difficulty with auditory information processing as a result of the stroke. I had no awareness of what this was or how this would affect my life. I could find no reference to its treatment for adult stroke victims in Australian research. I added this disorder into my overseas reading list from the Internet.

As I began to source research articles on this topic, I didn't fully realise that in many environments where there was high volume noise and reverberation from speakers, my brain had lost the ability to interpret and differentiate sound efficiently and instantaneously.

While in hospital, I was vaguely aware that when the HPs spoke to me from a distance in the noisy ward environment, or from behind me, their words sounded muffled and unintelligible. I didn't understand why, but put it down to the high level of surrounding noise in the ward during the day.

I frequently asked HPs to repeat what they said or what they asked me to do during their tests. From their body language, I had quickly learned that this was frustrating for them. I also realised that it was easy to understand what they said when they were in front of me, or during the quiet of the night when there was little environmental noise competing with a conversation. Even with the barrage of assessments conducted by various HPs, my auditory processing disorder was not mentioned anywhere in my file. It was not diagnosed, discussed or treated.

At my next visit to Ken, after receiving the results from some blood tests, he referred me for repeat testing, as my blood glucose seemed to be very high. In response to his query, I assured him that I wasn't diabetic.

At that meeting we talked about organising a new speech therapist. I was sceptical about therapists of any kind. But Heather had already tracked down a community-based speech therapist and given me her details for Ken. Within a few minutes he had arranged a visit from Adele for several weeks later.

Ken also arranged for me to have contact with a new neurologist. My only demand of him was that this would be a person who was respectful to his patients, given my earlier experience in hospital. His first choice in Keith was all that I hoped. My subsequent meetings with him showed him to be a person of integrity, honesty and optimism.

*

I had so far enjoyed my early morning walk each day, though I found it difficult to think about anything other than the stroke and my loss of language. Even at this stage I could feel myself becoming anxious—and probably raising my blood pressure—if I thought too much about my hospital experience. I practised self-discipline by clearing my thoughts of that experience and starting to enjoy the sounds and activities of life around me.

As I walked further around my community I began to gain a new appreciation of life: spider webs glistening in the winter sunlight tattered from the previous night's battles between the creatures of the night; more than 100 cockatoos noisily planning their day in their regular morning meeting on the electrical wires; aromas of toast wafting from homes; sounds of different car engines; and the chatter of students on their way to school.

In accordance with strategies used by some overseas therapists working with auditory processing disorders, I began to practise retraining my brain to listen and differentiate sounds around me—to be selective and focus on some, while ignoring others.

Initially, it was very difficult. I couldn't seem to work out what to focus on or the origin of sounds, such as cars travelling behind me that had passed before my brain could register the sound. Birdcalls became particularly useful. They were frequent, spontaneous and never the same. I couldn't see where the sound came from so as I approached various trees, I concentrated on locating their sound until I had passed the tree.

I began to speak, in a conversational way, to the magpies that invariably chattered to each other, and to the plovers that warned me away from their nests. I responded sympathetically to dogs who pleaded with me to take them for a walk and practised speaking to them in different ways: reassuringly, friendly, sternly, and happily, to re-acquaint my brain with alternative ways of speaking. I listened to my words, practising them repeatedly. On many occasions, I was the only person walking at that time of the morning, so I felt no inhibitions about talking to myself and the birds and animals as I walked.

Although I felt no embarrassment with my fractured language with my friends, I managed to avoid speaking to other walkers in case I failed even a simple greeting and couldn't think quickly enough to respond. But my first disaster inevitably occurred.

One morning, a neighbour out for a walk stopped me with a greeting, and her body language indicated that she wanted to chat. I panicked and couldn't remember her name, though I had known her for many years. I think she remarked on the weather but my brain couldn't follow her friendly conversation beyond my recognition of a few words. I smiled in response to her greeting, but I was consumed by my fear. *What if she asks me a question?* Then she did. I couldn't understand what she asked, so I blabbered incoherently something about having to get home quickly and turned and headed back as fast as I could. I was embarrassed and tearful. I knew she couldn't understand my response and she must have thought my behaviour was peculiar, particularly as she was heading in the same direction. *Will I ever be able to speak spontaneously and coherently again?* The next day, I left home for my walk earlier than usual and took a different route to avoid anyone that might speak to me.

When I returned home, it occurred to me that in avoiding interacting with other walkers, I was beginning to isolate myself. At the time it had seemed a better alternative than failing in a spontaneous conversation. I realised that this could be detrimental to my recovery, so I resolved to walk on routes where I may need to speak with other people, and have the courage to respond as best I could.

I ventured further from home each day by adding another block, the length of the football field or coming home a different way, feeling good in my efforts with no sign of another stroke. I also noticed that I had lost almost three kilos. I was feeling pleased with myself.

Almost four weeks after my exit from hospital, Ken suggested that I start driving carefully around my local community during quiet times, to regain my confidence. I was very afraid of this task and dismissed it to be considered at a later time. Barb had made sure that I was well stocked with food and drove me to appointments, so I had avoided the need to drive.

Then next day it was cold and raining. My elderly dogs and I loved the comfort and warmth of the fireplace in winter. Then during the afternoon, I discovered that the kindling had become wet from the rain and I had run out of firelighters (written as 'fire fighters' in my diary). As the afternoon wore on, I wondered if I had the courage and skill to drive to my local grocery store to buy some. As dogs do, they looked at me and at the fireplace, asking in their quiet, but not-so-subtle way, "What are you going to do about it?"

It took me almost two hours to muster the courage to make the trip. The light was fading quickly. In making the decision to drive, I convinced myself that as it was a Saturday afternoon, there was unlikely to be much traffic in my little village. As I slowly reversed two or three metres through the doors of the garage, I immediately discovered that my fragile brain couldn't perform this task using the car's mirrors. So I reversed a further metre or two, and then opened the car door to check that I was reversing in a straight line parallel to the fence. I repeated this action many times to reach the front gate and the road.

I drove slowly to the shops and finally parked the car outside the local IGA. Aware of my heart pounding, I picked up a red shopping basket at the door. I opened my wallet to check that I had sufficient money, and placed it into the basket. Gathering a few items including the firelighters, I proceeded to the checkout and unloaded the goods onto the counter. I returned the red basket near the door, almost colliding with another customer reaching for it from the stack.

I returned to the counter and within a few seconds I heard someone speaking to me. I saw that it was the other customer. I panicked. I didn't expect to speak to a stranger. I didn't answer and avoided his gaze. His voice became louder and more insistent as he held up the red basket near my face, and repeated his question, "Is this yours?" I felt my heart beating very fast by this stage. I felt flushed and embarrassed and burst into tears. *What do I say? My brain won't speak!* I quickly looked into the basket and noticed that there was 60c lying in the bottom of the basket, possibly having fallen out of my opened wallet. My language deserted me again, so I quickly handed over $5 for the firelighters and rushed out leaving the other items (and the 60c) on the counter. My last recollection of that incident was the startled look on the checkout operator's face as I ran from the shop, as he said, "That's weird!"

I drove home unable to stop the tears and the tide of emotions that swept over me: sense of loss, defeat, futility, frustration and humiliation. *How can I ever regain my ability to talk to people spontaneously? This is just too hard!*

The following day, I woke still hurting from my venture into the community. But sleep enabled me to now think more clearly through the incident. I had failed in a spontaneous conversation, but at least I had driven my car again. That was success! Then as I set about activities for the day, I realised that I needed to replenish more supplies for my dogs and me. This required a trip to a local shopping centre in the next suburb.

Thinking about this task raised my anxiety again. I knew I had to overcome my fear as quickly as possible. *But how?* Then I thought about scripting my responses to predictable questions that could arise at the supermarket from checkout operators, 'How are you today?' 'Do you have any fly buys?' I could answer them in one or two words. I also set up simple questions that I could ask unsuspecting sales assistants, so I could practise interacting confidently with someone that I didn't know. My plan was to practise the question until it was fluent. For example, 'Could you tell me where to find the couscous?' *Listen to her response. Then thank her with a smile.*

A few minutes of practice on my script before I set out from home, enabled me to say the question and response, without stumbling, in a timely way. It didn't seem so hard after all. *But can I do it as well in practice?*

The drive to the supermarket was another challenge. I tried to visualise the trip from home, and found it difficult to think through the route that I had travelled hundreds of times. *Is this my lack of confidence stopping me from thinking clearly? Have I lost the ability to plan even a familiar task?* I didn't allow myself to think too long about this dilemma. I grabbed my wallet, went to the garage, reversed the car a little more confidently than the previous day, focused on the task at hand, and set off from home. I divided the trip into sections. *Drive down the hill and turn left. Drive to the intersection and turn right…*

As I reacquainted my memory with each segment of a journey that had previously been so familiar, I could almost feel the little pathways in my brain 'clinking' into place.

At the supermarket, I practised my question when I reached the car park. I walked (looking, but not feeling) confidently inside. I took a couple of deep breaths and asked my couscous question. I couldn't follow the sales assistant's words as she led me to the couscous in the noisy environment of the supermarket, but her voice tone was friendly and informative with no questions. I was relieved. I thanked her with a smile. I dared to believe that scripting may be a useful tool to enable me to interact in the community, at least in survival tasks.

The following week, knowing that I was to meet Adele, the community-based speech therapist, I applied to the hospital to retrieve a copy of my medical file under Freedom of Information. I specifically asked for the return of the sheets that were snatched from my belongings by the HP as I was leaving. I thought it could be useful for Adele to know what progress I had made in the previous weeks from my early attempts in the hospital. When I received the medical file a few days later, the sheets weren't there. Following the advice of the hospital I wrote a specific letter requesting the sheets. A letter arrived from the HP's Manager in which she stated, "The incident didn't happen". I phoned her, queried her efforts in finding the sheets and challenged the veracity of the HP's denial of the incident that had taken place. She insisted that I was mistaken. I was very angry that an HP would deliberately lie to cover her spiteful behaviour, with no further investigation by her Manager.

I read every word and every line in the medical file over the next few days. I was appalled. It seemed that stroke victims must rarely retrieve their files. I couldn't believe the number of inaccuracies in assessments, errors in data, value judgments, poorly written reports, significant spelling errors, omissions, contradictions, and negativism on which HPs had apparently made their decisions about my care. There were many questionable or wrong entries in my file. I was devastated. *How could they have made valid decisions based on these poor quality reports?*

The following week I had an introductory meeting with Adele. Although she greeted me warmly, I was defensive, and immediately told her that I was concerned that I would be back to dealing with irrelevant assessments and exercises. Adele quickly assured me that she worked differently to conventional strategies. She asked if I would be happy for our meetings to travel through conversations about my 'life journey'. She explained how she could walk with and guide me, to reclaim those functional areas of my language that had been dismantled through the stroke. Within minutes I felt trust in her and her approach. Heather had been astute in her diligence in finding the right person to assist me. I looked forward to her second visit the following week.

She began that day with learning to regulate my breathing. She encouraged me to be conscious of using my breathing in phrasing to slow down my language. This reduced the stumbling that led to frustration, contributed to my anxiety, and increased my blood pressure. She suggested taking my BP, completing her breathing exercises then taking my BP again, so I could see their benefit. After her visit, I began to work on regulating my breathing while walking, aligning my steps to my breathing—in for two and out for two—to regain the rhythm.

Adele quickly recognised that there were some other physical issues that were inhibiting the recovery of my language: poor sleep patterns, frequent tiredness, and tightness in my chest, especially when I became frustrated with my fractured words. Through her 'big picture view' these were clearly important factors for me in recovering functional language.

When I mentioned that I was expert at using short naps to help me keep working, she tactfully explained that this was also a destructive habit. On her suggestion, I started working for shorter sessions before a break, and going to bed at the same time each night without music on the radio, as I drifted into sleep. I gradually began to engage in physical activity around the house as a distraction during the day—anything to avoid napping when I felt fatigued or stressed from work. Remedying this behaviour was harder than I thought. It was a habit that took significant willpower and time to achieve.

After reading information on building good sleep patterns, I removed the digital alarm clock with its luminous numbers from the bedroom, turned off the kitchen light that provided a distant glow in the event that I woke, and rearranged my work schedule to avoid using any form of electronic devices, within about half an hour before going to bed.

Through my meetings with Adele, I felt comfortable in disclosing and discussing my personal fears about my recovery from stroke. It was easy to talk with her openly and productively, in an approach that had no resemblance to the clinical approach I had previously experienced.

From the first session, she took a more holistic approach to assessment. She taught me to recognise how my language changed in response to day-to-day activities, my energy levels, and my breathing, especially if I was stressed or angry. At the end of our session, she gave me positive feedback on the improvements that I was showing, and gentle guidance about how to work on those areas that caused me concern or frustration.

We also talked about how to relax. This was an issue to which I had paid little attention even before the stroke. Adele suggested reading some fiction and historical biographies for a few minutes before going to sleep. I had missed this much-loved activity over the years while in business. I went to my local library and spent a delightful couple of hours wandering around and soaking up the environment of a modern library. I found a biography of Anne Boleyn in which there were many unfamiliar names, historical facts and tangled relationships. It was intriguing, and a good test of my ability to comprehend written language. The challenge was to remember the facts from one page to the next.

I started enthusiastically, but found that I could only read a few paragraphs before feeling overwhelmed by the dense language and the complexities that had characterised Ann Boleyn's life with Henry VIII. Each night, I found that I could rarely remember what I had read the night before. I began doing a recap out loud before reading, and focused on remembering the characters' names, incidents and relationships to re-acquaint me with the storyline. When I completely failed in remembering, I went back and re-read the previous few pages.

Adele was pleased with my resumption of relaxed reading and suggested journalling what I had read in brief notes each night, to improve my memory and concentration. This worked well in practising my paraphrasing, collating my thoughts and building my skills in following the threads of a story. It was slow-going and took several weeks to finish the book. But it was an enjoyable respite from reading clinical articles.

I also set up a jigsaw, a long forgotten hobby that I had loved for as long as I could remember. During the evenings, when my concentration for working was gone, I began to spend time with some music in 'quiet time' while working on my jigsaw to assist my brain to relax before sleep. I used the jigsaw to practise my organisational and prioritising skills to set up a system for its completion. This was a non-threatening, non-pressured and enjoyable way of problem-solving. It involved linking objects or ideas, sequencing, spatial relationships, deductive reasoning, comparison, rational thinking and logic—all skills that I knew were damaged to some degree by the stroke. I also found thousands of free jigsaws on the Internet that I could adjust to various levels of difficulty in an instant, for a break at any time of the day.

By using the tools from my environment that I treasured, these activities motivated me to re-build them into my life, while recovering my skills in reading, concentration, comprehension and analysis.

*

It was several weeks after coming home from hospital before I attended to some unopened personal mail. I found a recall letter from local BreastScreen services following a mammogram six days before the stroke. I wasn't perturbed, since I had received two recalls in previous years, both negative. But a day later, another more strongly-worded letter arrived, urging me to contact them urgently. Barb rang to arrange the appointment for me for the following day. I was a little concerned, having not received this type of letter before.

The following day, I underwent an ultrasound and a biopsy, showing that I almost certainly had breast cancer. I felt numbed. It was more than I could comprehend. Now I couldn't focus on anything but the cancer. The stroke recovery seemed to pale into insignificance as my brain and my comprehension shut down at this new diagnosis. I struggled between the nightmare I thought I was experiencing, and from which I couldn't wake, and the reality that I must be seriously ill, even though I didn't feel sick.

A few days later the cancer diagnosis was confirmed. Heather accompanied me to meet David, the Oncology Surgeon, who carefully and in a compassionate way, gave me some alternatives. But my preferred choice, a bilateral mastectomy, was not one of them. He gently, but firmly, explained how the enormity of this operation could increase the risk of a second stroke. He also emphasised the need to deal with the cancer quickly to avoid its potential spread. Knowing that my brain would remember little of what he had explained, Heather wrote down the answers to my questions during the appointment. With my injured brain reeling from this discussion, I couldn't think through the alternatives clearly to make a decision about which was best.

The brick wall arose again shielding my brain from the need to make decisions. But my anxiety was rising, as I knew I had to make a quick decision with limited capacity.

At my next visit to Ken two days later, he began with breaking the news of the confirmed diagnosis of Type II Diabetes. I said, "I have something even better than that —I have breast cancer."

In the next few seconds of silence, I didn't know whether to laugh or cry. What I thought was only one mountain to climb, even two, now there were three! We talked about the alternatives that David had discussed, and I finally understood the rationale for his suggestion for lumpectomy. I went home loaded with resources from the Cancer Council and the diabetes industry in some kind of a daze. *Will I die soon? Is there any point in trying to recover the stroke? Is it futile for me to try to work?* My scrambled brain found it too difficult to comprehend, and retreated into disbelief. I felt that I was closer to dying than I had felt before, even at the depths of my despair in hospital. I went to bed and slept for several hours to hide from the world.

When I woke, the memory of my visit to Ken's Clinic was still there. I tried to distract myself by watching television. But my brain now seemed to be more scrambled, my thoughts racing with no order or resolution. I couldn't concentrate. I couldn't understand what people were saying on the screen, and I couldn't think logically through any actions. For the first time in recent weeks it seemed like a hopeless situation, after working so hard and as positively as I could. I was devastated beyond tears. My mind was in a confusion that swirled around like a thick fog.

I contacted Heather and Annette to let them know about the diabetes diagnosis. Again, they were both shocked. But as always, they supported me with the warmth and optimism they had shown me on every occasion when I needed to talk. With their practical approaches and their reassurance that they were there for me in dealing with these new challenges, I dismissed the momentary idea that I could let nature take its course. I decided to fight! But I felt worn out from the previous few weeks in my effort of clambering towards success. Now I had lost my way in my journey. For the second time in a few short weeks I was aware of my lack of capacity to think about where to begin.

That afternoon, during my conversation with Adele, I exhausted myself with trying to come to terms with how to deal with these illnesses. My diary records how I felt that my language was 'sloppy', I frequently stumbled, and my voice sounded like it was 'outside my head'. I struggled to concentrate for more than a few minutes and my motivation was gone. Adele's gentle reassurance suggested that what I saw as a calamity could be an opportunity. At that time I couldn't agree, even though she was positive and genuine in her manner. Knowing that I had never sought solace in any faith we laughed when she suggested that, "The universe might be trying to tell you something".

As I set out for my walk the following morning, I began to think of the enormity of the situation. *How can I solve these problems?* My thoughts were racing from one issue to another and I couldn't focus on my auditory exercises while I walked. The life activities that I had enjoyed observing so much each morning now meant nothing. I felt like I hadn't made any progress at all.

But I must have walked at a fast pace for the most part, because as the endorphins kicked in, I felt my mood changing and by the time I returned home I had decided that I needed to find a role model, paradigm, template, procedure or framework —anything— to help me organise my life and give me some direction!

To begin, I wondered what my life would be like for the next few months. How many medical appointments for stroke, cancer and diabetes would I have, knowing that I would also soon have cancer surgery and 25 days of radiation therapy. For almost six hours I worked very slowly to set up a simple spreadsheet. It revealed a total of 82 appointments that I could predict—recognising that there could also be other unexpected ones. *This is logistically impossible! I will not spend my life in doctors' surgeries! What can I do?*

Over most of that weekend, I spent many hours trying to think or search the Internet to find any information on relevant recovery programs. I looked for a practical, understandable guide to give me some direction. But in my state of heightened anxiety —or hopelessness—I could find nothing to deal with these three illnesses together. *Perhaps there is nothing!* I spent a very restless night with little sleep.

I knew that what I needed was a different way of thinking. *But what is it?* I knew that my limited ability to think laterally, as a result of the stroke, was holding me back. *Am I looking at the wrong information?*

As I sat at the computer for another session of searching, I wondered if any of my clients could give me some inspiration. Many were highly successfully in their careers. I began to look for the high achievers. There were so many that I had worked with over the previous 25 years, across all occupations, from many parts of the world. *What are the commonalities among these high achievers? How do they achieve their targets time after time? What keeps them striving for their personal best each day?* I began to select categories of clients among those whose careers had focused on achievements: business, engineering, sales, sport, dance, music, research and several others. It was inspiring to read their histories again, and to reflect on the way that I had guided and collaborated with them in building their career pathways, sometimes through complicated journeys. I

Chapter Four

The Project

I knew from many of my clients' links with the health system over many years, that these three branches of medicine—stroke, cancer and diabetes—wouldn't 'speak' to each other. They certainly didn't want to speak to me. Through my battle in stroke services, I had been made to feel that I had lost my intelligence, so why would they bother?

Against the odds I was determined to succeed, and along the way prove them wrong. I felt rapidly growing anticipation at the prospect of overcoming these illnesses, which heightened my desire to take control of my life again. I spoke excitedly to Ken about my plan.

I proposed to follow the model of so many of my engineering clients: the perfectionists, the never-say-die leaders and problem-solvers. I knew that creativity was part of their systematic approach to achieving their project outcomes. This aligned Bloom's Taxonomy. I remembered that rather than being bound to traditional principles, some of my clients saw innovation and creativity as their guiding principle. I had learned that they worked by the concept: 'there is always an alternative'. This had also been my mantra when working in business, and with clients' complex needs in their careers. *I will deal with these illnesses like a 'project'.*

Ken didn't judge my idea negatively, though I detected a glimpse of hesitation, especially as I suggested that I would be the Project Manager and he would be the 2IC. I knew that I would invariably need to have at least some contact, even indirectly, with HPs for the foreseeable future. I saw his role as the conduit between them and me. At least they would talk to him. I could collate the documentation from each HP supplier, so I could track my progress. But I understood that his approach was necessarily a conservative one.

Even with his guarded support, I went home with a new sense of vigour. Over the next few hours, I looked through many documents that I had constructed for my engineering clients. I selected a few outstanding examples as models to take the first steps towards setting up my project

Although I had shown a brave face to Ken, I strived to visualise the whole project with a fragile brain struggling to form linkages between ideas. *How will I know that I'm on the right track?* I knew I needed a framework that was flexible enough to accommodate the unknown problems that were likely to occur. *Can this work? What if it fails?*

My hesitation reminded me that I had not yet recovered that elusive higher level of analysis and conceptual thinking that I had previously used in my work. I needed to regain these skills and my ability to 'see the big picture'. This had been such a critical part of running the administrative side of my business, and when working with my clients.

While thinking through some ideas, I realised that there were many differences between recovery from illness, and those tangible engineering outcomes such as building a ship, a state-of-the-art aircraft, an Olympic sporting venue or constructing a major highway. *How do I measure the intangibles of well-being, self-confidence and resilience?*

But I knew that I couldn't be daunted by these differences. The project strategies used by my engineering clients had provided at least some direction on the long road ahead. I accepted that there would sometimes be deviations that I couldn't control, and perhaps some outcomes that may never be achieved. Others needed refocusing to be more realistic. But as I couldn't identify them as unachievable at this stage, I decided to proceed anyway.

I also knew that a critical area of project management was planning. I could see in my clients' approaches to their tasks, that they had asked themselves many questions prior to commencing their respective projects. I did the same. I needed to identify the barriers and risks that I could expect to encounter and set up a plan to manage them. *What can I do to efficiently integrate recovery from stroke, cancer treatment and diabetes management? With the enormity of the project, how can I avoid another stroke from potential stress, particularly within the first six months? What costs will be involved? Who will I use as suppliers of the services I will need, given my misgivings about HPs? How will I maintain the stamina and inner strength to continue, if necessary, for years?*

I knew that my measure of success was in answering these questions for myself. I wanted to be independent again, to make choices in my life based on considered decisions and outcomes in order to maintain my motivation. I had to avoid being consumed and influenced by marketing, ideas of well-meaning but uninformed people and/or those who sought to have power through negativism.

When I took the plunge to set up my business many years ago, someone said to me, "Surround yourself with positive people and never look back!" When I dealt with the pessimists over the years, I had recalled this statement many times. Now it became the foundation of my recovery.

Chapter Five

Project Planning:
Co-ordinating the Resources

Through brainstorming—no pun intended—I tentatively began to consider all the issues involved, to find some way of categorising them. As the list grew longer, I realised there were so many—perhaps I'd even missed some. My thoughts became jumbled and I couldn't think clearly to categorise them in some order. I needed to identify the many programs or elements that would be required within the project. *Can I really do this with my fractured brain? Have I been unrealistic in taking this path? What if I fail?*

I knew that I needed systems and tools to monitor what I was doing to prove to Ken (and me) that my project was feasible and working. I also knew that it needed something simple, as my brain would likely falter in trying to remember or deal with complex processes.

I began compiling a Project Plan to set out the issues under 'stroke', 'cancer' and 'diabetes'. I set up several charts for recording those activities that would give me relevant data that I could see quickly, and modify my activities and tasks as necessary.

I set up a simple table to record daily weight, blood pressure, waist measurements, BMI and blood glucose. This also gave me repetitive use of simple mathematics including daily calculations and interpreting numbers. (Later, I extended this table to record many other physical data). I used my electronic diary for daily schedules, maintained my personal diary to record problems and successes, and set up a record of telephone calls and conversations from HPs regarding appointments and telephone calls. I also compiled copies of all records and reports from Ken and specialist doctors, reading them carefully and educating myself on their content and data. These simple monitoring activities, completed each day, reduced the stress involved in any potential memory loss and gave me practice in using a range of skills in prioritising, organising, and concentrating on detail.

I also set up a Stroke Words Chart in which I listed many of the stumbles that occurred, the context in which they occurred, and my corrections. By recording these incidents frequently, it gave me practice in listening for and recognising my errors, and seeing if the frequency of my stumbles were reducing. Some of them were very interesting, to say the least!

Extract from Stroke Words Chart (during a conversation with Annette):

I said:	I should have said:
'The MRI showed that I didn't have a genital problem.'	'The MRI showed that I didn't have a congenital problem.'

We laughed at that one!

Identifying the scope of the project was taxing mentally and physically. I couldn't work out how to set deadlines, targets or timelines for these illnesses to know that I had achieved real and quantifiable outcomes. I didn't know enough about how long it took to lose weight or how much to lose, how to recover my language to my pre-stroke level, how to reduce diabetes, how to recover from cancer surgery or respond if the cancer returned.

I had no prior personal experience to draw on ideas or strategies to help me. So I decided to discard the abundant pessimistic research and use only reference material that seemed positive, valid research and was practical in its implementation. I easily found a plethora of reports emphasising that a positive approach—physically and mentally—was clearly beneficial to dealing with all three illnesses. To begin my project without delay, I set broad pathways to give me some direction, knowing that they could change with the uncertainty of these illnesses and my successes:

1. Manage the diabetes.
2. Minimise the recurrence of the cancer.
3. Reduce the likelihood of another stroke.

The engineers that I looked to for my inspiration highlighted risk management as a key element in achieving their targets. *What are the risks that could hinder my progress?* Then as best I could, given my impaired analytical skills, I identified some ways for me to mitigate the risk:

Risk:

High probability of recurrence of stroke from cerebral haemorrhage and other complications such as seizures within six months

Solution:

- Recognise and reduce those emotional or work-based activities or situations that could lead to hypertension and stress
- Improve diet and exercise.
- Work systematically with frequent breaks.
- Regulate sleep.

Risk:

High blood sugar that could increase the likelihood of a further stroke and lead to many other physical illnesses associated with diabetes.

Solution:

- Change diet and increase exercise. Link these elements into a regular, functional schedule.
- Regulate sleep.
- Manage hypertension.

Risk:

Recurrence and spread of cancer

Solution:

- Surgery to minimise the likelihood of spread.
- Improve diet and exercise for general health and well-being, and assist in coping with radiation treatment.
- Stay positive and motivated.

Clearly the common factor was diet and exercise—I could easily deal with those myself. There were no real barriers. Whatever I did in this area to change my current situation was going to be beneficial. Even with my reduced cognitive ability, I could see that it was entirely my responsibility.

Plunging into education about the causative factors of these illnesses highlighted the little I had really known about them. As I ramped up my reading, I realised that I had lived in an illusion about my knowledge of a healthy lifestyle gained from easy reading in magazines and media reports. I knew I had to gain more deeper knowledge—and in so doing, I began a new pathway of discovery that led me into an Aladdin's Cave.

I looked to see what I could do *immediately*, to start the process. I had already learned that hypertension is often called the 'quiet killer'—with unrecognised symptoms that I had dismissed as tiredness. I had paid little attention to relaxation or time off work. Working hard with few breaks was an expected downside of small business. So I built quiet time into each day for planning and monitoring the project. I worked for shorter periods before a few minutes' break, adhered to dietary improvement, continued to monitor my weight and integrated regular exercise into my daily schedule. This became the framework for building new daily routines.

Recovering my comprehension was less measurable, but the process was essential to finding and interpreting information that I could follow. In a few weeks I had made some significant gains that were evident in my emails:

> *Email to Annette, 5 weeks post-stroke:*
> *"I'm keeping my diary each day—I can't follow many conversations on the phone. Better at expressive communication but struggling with receptive. This is harder so I have to make judgments and decisions. Can't really interpret comedy—it looks funny, but is meaningless. I watched the generations show that I've never seen before—but I couldn't work out won!"*

Although I desperately wanted to speak and write fluently again, as quickly as possible, I realised that even with some gains, there was a long way to go. Every action and interaction had to be purposeful in rebuilding my skills.

I found that speaking on the phone was difficult without the visual cues of the speaker. Bernard assisted me by recording a phone message suggesting callers use email, to maintain communication with my clients. This reduced the stress associated with trying to conduct phone conversations.

Adele took the different moods and emotions that I brought to each meeting in her stride. At times I was frustrated and angry with myself, because I felt that I wasn't improving my language quickly enough. We talked many times about my expectations of myself. She didn't see my plan as unrealistic, but recognised that my frustrations arose from a different source. We often talked, even laughed, about the 'p' word—'patience'—that had never been one of my attributes.

What I particularly admired and respected about Adele was her guidance in rebuilding my skills in problem-solving. She empowered me to make my own decisions with confidence. This meant that I was less stressed and my language was more coherent. She discussed, negotiated and suggested, but never directed me around the issues in my recovery and my work.

Following one of our conversations, I strategically placed writing pads throughout my home. In any room, I could note something immediately and reduce my fear of forgetting or overlooking important tasks or information. Within another month, I had replaced the writing pads with an iPad that I kept with me at all times. This became extremely useful and accelerated my recovery through its portability: when writing notes, cooking in the kitchen, accessing the Internet from anywhere, making better use of the daily diary, being in the garden, and while shopping. I used it as a storage vehicle for my music, saving the need for a heavy music bag, and for jigsaws when I needed some relaxation or retraining my brain when away from home.

There were also simple techniques Adele suggested to deal with the auditory processing disorder. I listened repeatedly to a voice on a CD reading a story, and gradually built my recognition of the sequence of words. She also transferred this technique to learning how to write down a telephone number left by clients on my phone. I played the message several times, listening and noting the numbers one-by-one in the sequence. She showed me how placing a blank sheet of paper under a line of hard copy of writing assisted my eyes to track the information more succinctly when reading aloud. This worked in the same way that I had discovered the value of using highlighted text on the computer screen. I could see on Bloom's Taxonomy that I had begun to climb the ladder towards my previous level. My simple monitoring systems and data sheets showed that my health was also steadily improving.

*

It was several weeks before I returned to choir rehearsal: the first time not to play, but just to be there. As I hadn't yet driven at night, Steven and his wife Anne, collected me from home. I went to rehearsal with a great sense of anticipation. I was welcomed warmly. I sat with the group and proceeded to sing with them. But the night was a disaster for me.

Immediately, I found that my skills had gone in the combined tasks of phrasing the words correctly in a song's rhythm, keeping time, listening to and following the melody and moving around key sections in the music. At home, I could play to my own rhythm and I hadn't tried to sing. I realised very quickly that with the sound of 60 voices and a piano echoing around me in the rehearsal hall, my brain couldn't interpret and differentiate the sounds of voice and instrument or keep up with the pace of even the slowest song. I faltered frequently in trying to read and follow the words. I had lost my pronunciation, tonality, rhythm and phrasing. I couldn't link sections of songs or recognise the 'music map' of the songs. I couldn't anticipate the sections, or the bridge, in songs that I knew well. It was a long two hours. I despaired and felt like I had failed again.

Feeling miserable later that night at home, I considered the prospect of having to leave the choirs, to concentrate on dealing with the illnesses. *Maybe it's all too much for me to imagine that I could return to accompany the choirs!* I didn't know how to tell Annette and John of my decision. So I delayed the inevitable. I told them I wasn't yet ready to come back to choir. I spoke to Heather and as always she gently urged me to take things more slowly and, "Give it time". She always put a practical focus on my anxieties and used her innate ability to talk me through things in a logical way, when my brain could see no pathway through the fog.

While cautiously believing that I could overcome the medical problems, it felt that relearning the range of music required for the choirs seemed to be an insurmountable hurdle.

However, after a few days of thinking I went back to playing piano, spurred by my desire to rekindle my love of music. I began songs slowly, section-by-section for a few minutes at a time throughout the day. I needed to identify the specific problems that were holding me back. I realised that I had lost my skills in conceptualising a lengthy piece of music, anticipating the next bar at page turns, automatically knowing the sections of a piece and thinking through introductions that weren't always written.

Counting beats and bars even for simple melodies was arduous. I often lost count and couldn't retain my concentration for more than a short time. *Is this a result of the loss of numerical skills through the stroke? Or is it my lack of self-confidence?* I was shocked that the skills that had come so naturally were at best sporadic, and at worst, gone.

I noticed that if I was tired, it was more difficult to interpret the music. So I rescheduled my practice sessions to the mornings where possible. It was logical that to achieve something—no matter how small—was more likely to occur while I was alert, than when I was tired. Until this time, I had used my breaks in an ad hoc way—whatever I could think to do at the time to be active. Now I needed to set up a functional program for break activities so that I dealt with them at opportune times. At the lowest level, they were high activity-based mixed with musical practice in the morning (exercise, playing piano, housework) complemented by less strenuous exercise (stretching, office tasks, food preparation) in the afternoons and evenings.

I desperately hoped that just as my language was returning through my intensive practice more quickly than predicted, so would my musical skills. Slowly, I began to hear some improvements, by going over difficult passages many times and sometimes note-by-note. I noticed that I could play through entire songs, with fewer mistakes, and my hopes grew. I tried to convince myself that it was only one more step to transferring what I had accomplished at home to the rehearsal room and gigs.

With a great deal of apprehension, eight weeks after the stroke, I returned to rehearsal. This time, it was to accompany the choirs. Being among friends and welcomed warmly into the positive and energetic atmosphere created by the singers, boosted my motivation to succeed.

Annette turned to me and announced the first song. I played the introduction confidently, but as soon as the singing started, I was swamped by a deafening cacophony of sound. After all my effort, I was completely unable to differentiate the sound of the piano from the singers' voices. I felt my anxiety rising and I was shocked that there seemed to be no difference from my first attempt several weeks earlier. My confidence plummeted. *What's the point in my hard work?* I despaired that I could never be their accompanist again.

I struggled through the rehearsal realising my inadequacy, and trying to make some sense of the music, but making more frequent mistakes. The only way to know if I was keeping up with the choir was to watch Annette conducting. But when I looked at her, away from the piano, I lost my place in the music. My brain couldn't work quickly enough to regain the place. I lurched through the music, trying to interpret the notes and keep up with the singers. I became flustered in trying to find my way around the music again. I had no idea how I played, but I knew it was nothing like my previous skills. I was miserable, while trying to keep a brave face. In their characteristic style, the singers were accepting and non-judgmental even though I had played badly. On that first night, I left for home with a severe headache and a heavy heart.

It took a great deal of effort to believe in myself after that experience. But from the next day, I went back to my practice with several short periods—knowing that I was getting better, at least at home. I surmised that my inability to read music was a function of the difficulty of my brain to quickly and fluently read and interpret written and auditory information—not a loss of skills in playing the piano. It also became obvious to me that my memory of how to play the vast repertoire of music that I had accumulated had disappeared—or at least was in my brain out of reach, and in a million pieces. The arrangements and improvisations developed over many years (but never written down) and played thousands of times, were severely diminished or gone. So I made sure that in my short sessions, I played something that I enjoyed and could play without effort, while also trawling page-by-page through the choir's repertoire to re-familiarise myself with the music. While I played, I could become lost in the music, more relaxed in my world and feel a sense of achievement. I began to work actively to avoid failure and forced myself to believe that things would improve.

*

Around this time, a client contacted me on behalf of a friend, who was struggling with his confidence for an upcoming job interview. I explained to him that a stroke had affected my language. But he reiterated that if I could manage to do the interview training with his friend, he knew it would give him the confidence he needed. I also saw this as a challenge, and a practical test of my effort in regaining my skills in running seminars and education programs. So I agreed—with great trepidation—to run the training the following week.

In the preceding days, I practised and rehearsed every section of the three-hour training program many times. I focused on slowing my language, improving my rhythm, and practising phrasing, to reduce black holes and stumbles. The training was also a good exercise in maintaining my concentration over a lengthy period.

I found thousands of limericks and tongue twisters on the Internet for drill, to intensify practising rhythmic breathing for smooth and confident speaking. Then I increased these skills by reading poetry, even Shakespeare, to improve the flow of my language.

Although I faltered occasionally on the day, the client was very grateful for my effort. I was exhausted at the end of the training, but felt satisfied that I had done my best. I was pleased with my success in lasting the distance during the training, without becoming stressed. His improved confidence was evident during the training—and showed in his interview. This was topped off with his success in gaining a job that had eluded him twice previously. It was an achievement for both of us.

This success gave me added motivation to proceed in my current pathway. I could easily practise simple limericks and short verses while walking, and I felt pleased with myself that after regular practice, I could remember five lines of verse. At this point—less than five months after the stroke—I stopped apologising for my stumbles. Adele was very pleased with this decision. It was a turning point, and I knew that I was well on track to find my way out of the fog, with at least this aspect of my project.

With renewed vigour, I reviewed, refined, tweaked and streamlined my timetable to accommodate the major activities that I needed to do daily and weekly. I needed to keep up the momentum and functional activities each day: work in my business, exercise, read aloud about health issues, practise piano and record health checks. I also made frequent changes and additions to my diet, attended regular appointments with Ken and Adele, maintained my home, took functional breaks throughout the day and cared for my beloved dogs. I also made time every night to do some jigsaw and/or read a novel before sleep. Just as my engineers had shown me, I learned that flexibility was important—but consistency was essential in keeping the project heading in the right direction.

From this time, I went back to weekly rehearsals for both choirs, even though my brain still struggled with the sound. William's help was invaluable in letting me know the next song that we were singing, or if we stopped to practise part of a song and my brain couldn't hear Annette's directions over the sound of the piano. As I often continued to play, oblivious to the interruption, a light tap on the arm let me know that the choir had stopped singing to learn a section. He became my 'ears', which helped my brain to slowly adjust to this environment, without panicking or feeling silly. I didn't know how long it would take me to regain my skills. But with each rehearsal I began to feel a little more confident, and William became expert in keeping me on track.

I found myself more closely reading the music for the first time in many years. Although I was familiar with almost all of the music from my days as a professional musician, many of the arrangements were different to what I knew. Throughout the years in accompanying the choirs, the music had served as a guide—without paying too much attention to the detail. Over time I became aware that I was improving in my technique, and quicker in interpreting the music. I often heard the music differently as the clarity and beauty of the sounds emerged, sometimes in short bursts, and sometimes after several days or weeks of practice. I spontaneously developed new improvisations. It was exciting and motivating!

For the first time since the stroke, I dared to believe that this was the re-emergence of my creativity. It was emerging through the soup of unintelligible noise and loss of sound differentiation that had characterised my early return to the choirs. I wanted to do the best that I could to justify the singers' faith in me, and complement their beautiful sound. I grasped this tiny lifeline to give me the pathway back to my music.

Chapter Six

Project Scope: Facing the Facts

I was learning that with my injured brain, there were difficulties in writing productively for long periods. This was particularly obvious when editing or writing complex documents to meet deadlines for my business clients. My previous speed and concentration was now severely diminished because of my slowed reading, writing and comprehension. This resulted in long workdays in writing, reading aloud, checking and rechecking often many times, reading slowly word-by-word, re-editing and polishing, line-by-line on and off the computer.

At times I became very tired and despondent if I felt that my work was falling behind. Sometimes I became apprehensive, with a lot of work still to do when getting close to deadlines. But when I faltered in a task, felt like giving up or doubted my capacity, I disciplined myself to work for one more minute, or one more paragraph, or one more page— or take a short break, and come back to do one more task. Sometimes, after a longer break, I had the concentration and strength to keep focused on the job for much longer, until I needed another break. After several months I had almost lost my dependence on short naps and had instead learned to do something active to regain my strength and concentration. This was also slowly helping me sleep better at night.

Frank had become astute in helping me to correct the unrecognised stumbles during our conversations. We had developed some simple systems for me to keep track of day-to-day tasks when he wasn't there. I sometimes faltered with financial calculations, so his expertise in this area meant that any problems were managed. I appreciated his diligence and meticulous attention to detail in checking my work.

*

I had never enjoyed housework but I now saw these tasks as opportunities. I could increase my daily activity level at no cost, with tools that required no preparation, but provided instant and accessible breaks from work. I coined the term 'Work Break Activities' (WBAs) to gain some positives out of what I saw as boring and repetitive jobs. There were literally dozens of WBAs that provided some way of becoming more active naturally—from making the bed, emptying the garbage, or sweeping the kitchen floor—in as long it took to make a cup of tea before heading back to work. I practised my music regularly to sprinkle a few minutes of musical joy through my day between less exciting WBAs.

But with the challenges ahead unfolding each day, it was easy to become distracted. With the often painstakingly slow pace involved in producing quality work, I took each minute of each day as it came, searching for any indication that I was improving—in anything. With each teachable moment, I continually asked myself: how can I improve that task? How can I work more efficiently? I worked hard to manage the project by integrating everything I did. I saw any little gains as successes.

I found that even with familiar procedures, my brain frequently encountered black holes that reduced my efficiency. Annette's sister Lorraine, with a strong administrative background, spent several days streamlining my business procedures. This was invaluable, as I now had simplified and efficient procedures to reduce the difficulty of remembering everything. This also meant Frank could more easily monitor the accuracy of my daily business activities. Greg, my accountant, and his staff Anne and Michaela, were always available to help as necessary.

*

I was an Obese Girl (OG). Dress size 22. 101kg. XXL. BMI 40. Waist 106cm.

Over the years of middle age, I had referred to myself as 'overweight'. I didn't want to admit the extent of my obesity, but now with three potentially life-threatening illnesses, I knew it had to be addressed if I was to survive. It was time to be honest with myself. Over the years I hadn't seriously tried to deal with being an OG, although at times I had hated myself. I denied myself the clothes that I really loved as 'punishment' for my lack of self-discipline or motivation to address the problem over the long term. I avoided photographs and mirrors and told myself that I could procrastinate until retirement. As most members of my family for at least two generations were obese, it was easier to believe that it was inevitable, rather than deal with the problem.

I had also learned to live with the many irritating physical problems resulting from obesity that women tend to accept as part of life. Rather than educate them on how to deal with the cause, these have fuelled a booming industry for pharmaceutical companies that have groomed women to expect these problems to occur, with expensive products and drugs to manage them.

Obese at the time of the stroke

Now, I was confronted with the consequences of years of complacency and denial. As I started to read more extensively, it seemed that my survival from any or all of these illnesses, was tied closely or indirectly to my weight loss. I needed to make simultaneous, major changes to exercise and diet—to sustain any improvement—for life.

Pre-stroke, exercise had not been a priority. As I had steadily gained weight through adulthood and middle age it was also harder to start to reduce the trend. The discomfort associated with exercise, as an OG, meant that I had avoided it.

Ironically, my daily walks since the stroke, gave me time to think about how best to deal with effective weight loss. They were already contributing to improved health.

I meticulously completed the measurements each day on my health spreadsheet, adding data such as BMR, type of exercise, exercise program changes, general health and daily steps. As well as providing data for Ken, this also gave me regular and functional practice in using numbers in different ways, using manual and electronic calculations to record BMI and BMR. The exercise for my body was also good exercise for my brain.

Within eight weeks, my chart showed that I had steadily lost eight kilos by walking and making some initial changes to my diet. My blood pressure was stable. This was the first time in my life that I had seen data highlighting my health status on paper. I felt cautiously pleased with myself, even though the weight loss wasn't yet very obvious, by any measures except on the data sheet. I realised that it was a long road moving from being an OG, to a Fat Girl (FG), and finally to a Healthy Girl (HG).

The information I read from many dietitians and researchers in Australia, suggested weighing yourself no more often than weekly or even monthly, 'to avoid disappointment'. I saw this as a pessimistic approach that sets people up to fail. I weighed myself at the same time every day, using mathematics to show trends and an indication of progress. But I could also see from my reading that weight was not a very reliable indicator of health. It was one of many tools available to monitor a healthy lifestyle.

Many researchers agreed that losing a kilo each week was achievable, safe and sensible. I worked diligently with my plan, and looked for the smallest sign of change on the scales by Tuesday. If there was none, I changed my food or my exercise, or both, to make it happen by Saturday. I learned that small portions in each meal were sufficient for my dietary needs, and I always made sure that I had enough food to cover my recommended daily intake of nutrients.

I found that on many websites (especially healthy recipe writers sponsored by food manufacturers), a serving size far exceeded what I required to maintain optimum health and feel satisfied at the end of a meal. So, if the recipe said, 'Serves 4' I divided the food into six or more meals. This also began to build a bank of frozen food of ready-made meals that could be prepared within a few minutes. This contributed to lower costs, with food almost free of additives, preservatives, sugar, salt, fat and chemicals.

I quickly learned that it was about the technique of slow eating—savouring and chewing 20 times, putting eating utensils down and resting from eating regularly through the meal. I was learning first-hand—becoming conscious of when it was happening—that boredom, stress or emotion was a trigger for eating. Drinking water or tea between meals frequently curbed the need to eat—especially if I felt hungry when I knew I shouldn't be, e.g. half an hour after a meal. I also significantly increased my water intake, another important factor in renewing my health. Sometimes I drew on an old-fashioned strategy for coping with temptation: 'Take a deep breath, have a drink of water, and do something else—away from the kitchen'.

I was now regularly walking for about an hour each day. *But am I walking the recommended 10,000 steps mentioned in many articles on exercise and fitness? What does 10,000 steps per day feel like—will*

I be exhausted? How much activity is that? Can I keep it up for life? I bought a pedometer at a local sport store, to find out.

I had assumed that my combined morning walk and regular WBAs were sufficient. I was wrong. The pedometer reading on the first day showed me that I accumulated around 5,000 steps on my regular walk and about 3,000 extra steps, during the rest of the day with WBAs.

To meet the recommended target, I had to exercise harder, with little extra time available in my tight daily schedule. I varied my program by extending my walking by an extra 15 minutes, and developed a scale of walking to give me more steps in the same time. It had three levels: 'Purposeful' (3 steps per second and can speak aloud for a sentence), 'Hurry' (4 steps per second and can only speak up to 4 words before becoming breathless) and 'Late' (5 steps per second and can't speak or sing). I divided my walk into sections incorporating all three paces, as a way of maintaining my motivation and providing in-built change in intensity in my walking activity.

Periodically, I used a graded walking program developed by a past US Olympic walking champion, Dave McGovern, where I could easily vary my walking activity. It was sometimes fatiguing yet surprisingly energising. I began to like the adrenaline rush resulting from physical achievement, and the feeling of what I termed, 'energised fatigue.'

I began wearing a backpack to add in weight so that I had to work harder to carry a heavier load, without any significant added time allocated to my walk. I steadily extended the periods that I walked at the Late pace until it became the majority of my walk, with an increasingly heavier backpack, for never less than an hour, every day. This pace was the real cardio exercise, evident in measuring my heart rate regularly, and the one that contributed most to my consistent weight loss.

I no longer avoided other early morning walkers by wearing sunglasses and large hats to avoid conversation. I began using people

I passed as an opportunity to smile and say, "Good morning—lovely day for a walk", with good rhythm, without stumbling.

While I knew I had made good gains in my language, I was still plagued with the auditory processing disorder. Unexpectedly during my walk, I discovered that the level at which my brain could interpret and differentiate sound in the environment was also influenced by whether or not I wore a hat. It was severely restricted if I wore a hat with a wide brim. So, where possible, I wore a sun visor for skin protection while maximising my brain's concentration on sounds around me.

To my dismay after exhaustive searching, I could find no available resources in Australia to assist me with this problem. Over several months I wrote, emailed and called many audiologists and their associations, researchers in universities and experts related to the field. I concluded that this disorder was ignored in Australia for adult stroke victims. Counselling seemed to be the only support vaguely offered by a few HPs, mentioned in a few websites.

*

I read that about 5% of the adult stroke population experiences this disorder along with loss of language. It is debilitating, socially isolating, and destroys confidence and self-esteem. It affects individuals in many different ways. Depending on proximity to the speaker, it sets up a tiring and sometimes embarrassing situation of asking others to repeat their conversation (often to the other person's annoyance), never quite getting the jokes or missing the threads of normal conversation. It prevents recognition and processing of key words and ideas, inability to respond to banter when speaking in a group or social situation, and struggling with complex concepts such as humour. It also contributes to what seems like forgetfulness as the brain fails to prioritise and act on key information.

Overseas, this is a very active field of research and a rapidly growing industry in its treatment. The overwhelming approach from overseas research deals with this disorder in a person's own environment, using functional strategies and easily accessible resources.

*

I found a number of strategies from several sources that I implemented and monitored for myself, which seemed to assist in some situations. During my walks I intensified my earlier attempts at training my brain to differentiate selective sounds from a noisy environment, without necessarily seeing the source. I expanded my attention from the sound, to include its function: birdcalls (are they near or far/moving or still/large or small birds?), engines (are they sedans/4 wheel-drives/petrol or diesel/small and large trucks/buses?), and voices (are they male/female, young/older people around me in busy shopping centres?). I counted how many seconds from when I first heard a car engine coming towards me from the front or rear, to when the sound faded. I concentrated on listening for as long as possible, and then moved smoothly to other sounds that took over from the engine noise. I diligently and intensively practised these techniques each morning for an hour and actively sought other, more spontaneous opportunities in other contexts during the rest of the day.

I continued to ask questions of unsuspecting sales assistants. I asked for directions to find products and costs of items to initiate conversation and gradually extended my interaction to include a comment on the product or its use in a recipe. This gave me practice in interpreting spontaneous sounds with different voices, language and accents. I concentrated as hard as I could, so I didn't have to ask for the information to be repeated. While I thought this was working well, I realised that on a number of occasions I had thanked people for their assistance in an odd way. Instead of saying, "Thank you so much", I suddenly realised that I had said several times, "Thank you much".

Once I recognised this error, I practised the phrasing and the rhythm needed for the correct sentence several times in my car before heading into the shopping centre. In this way I eliminated the error completely and thanked them with confidence. *A little more of the fractured jigsaw in my brain, falling into place!*

I also concentrated on listening to voices, with varying success, making announcements on PAs in shopping centres. I initiated very light conversation with the checkout operators with greetings and simple comments about it being 'a busy day'. In that way I had to initiate and conduct a conversation in a noisy environment, even if it was the same conversation each time. Fortunately for them, they were generally different people each day.

Chapter Seven

Project Action: Changing Mindset

Within a few days of the diagnosis of diabetes, I had begun extensive reading on 'managing diabetes', the term used by most Australian resources. This highlighted the need for a focus on balancing nutrients, small meal portions with regular eating and exercise patterns. Much of this material also stated or inferred that once diagnosed, diabetes was here to stay. As I knew very little about diabetes, I reluctantly accepted what I saw as a negative prognosis.

It was obvious that my horrendous pre-stroke workload, obesity, lack of functional exercise, and frequent eating to maintain my energy through long days and nights without sleep, had been major factors in my deteriorating health and the development of this treacherous disease.

With the diagnosis also came the need for regular testing of blood glucose. While it was only mildly uncomfortable to perform this task, I could foresee it becoming an annoyance in the long term. *Will my difficulty in following procedures result in forgetfulness in testing if away from home for any length of time? Will I be sticking pins in my fingers for life?* I realised that this would require considerable planning to always have testing equipment and the right food available, at the right time. I was also stunned at the aggressive marketing of designer testing and associated equipment. I saw being diabetic as potentially very expensive. I imagined being caught up in a perpetual cycle that could not be missed, without potentially dire consequences. I felt like a captive consumer!

Then as I started to download more information about diabetes, I found that overseas research often talked about 'reversing' Type II Diabetes. I couldn't understand the difference in the terminology.

The words 'management' and 'reversal' signalled entirely different approaches. More reading indicated that it was possible to reverse it with apparently no more effort required than management. But the outcomes were potentially vastly different. 'Manage' kept it there; 'reversal' meant not having it. The key was with a different mindset and a more positive approach.

I began to compare these different approaches. I found an undercurrent of hopelessness inferred by many HPs in Australia about people's capacity to change their behaviour about healthy eating. There were frequent messages with the advice to reduce intake of foods high in sugar, fat and sodium and to have small amounts, 'so you don't feel that you are missing out'. I found this advice negative, demotivating and unhelpful. It inferred that the unhealthiest foods laced with sugar, salt, fat, preservatives and additives, were the most enjoyable, but not advised for diabetics. In reality, these very accessible unhealthy choices are promoted by aggressive marketing as 'short cut', 'convenient', 'easy to prepare' and 'time saving'. These are powerful arguments in our busy lives.

During a casual discussion with one of my clients who was working as a dietitian, this negative mindset about weight loss was obvious. She stated:

> "Anyone can lose weight if they only have an intake of 1200 calories per day. But the food is so boring at that level, we know people won't stick to the diet plan. So it doesn't last and they put more weight back on. It's not sustainable so they give up."

I was dismayed when I read about the resources and support that was available to me as a newly diabetic patient. This involved a large team of HPs (up to 13 people!) with multiple appointments each year, and a boring and uncreative dietary plan from the Diabetes Council containing a significant percentage of processed foods. This seemed to be unhealthy eating from the outset. Even with my injured brain I could see that this was a no-win situation and for many people was doomed to fail. I could see diabetes management looming as a treadmill that could severely restrict me in my desire to maximise my health outcomes. It would be disempowering by being at the mercy of a highly fractured health system, and spending the majority of my time visiting HPs.

I realised that among HPs working in diabetes, a dietitian knows a lot about the food, a podiatrist knows a lot about feet and an eye doctor knows about eyes. But it seemed to me that integrating the support for an individual with Type II diabetes seemed cumbersome, time consuming and destined for failure with the highly fractured nature of HP disciplines that don't communicate with each other. Even with a GP as skilled as Ken, the treadmill was never going to achieve for me what I needed. *Why manage diabetes when I could get rid of it?*

With no evidence that I had permanent or irreparable damage caused by the diabetes, I changed my strategy from: '*Manage* the diabetes' to:

'*Reverse* the diabetes'.

I began compiling well-written overseas research articles and reading websites with a positive focus on reversal. As far as possible, I searched for information that didn't seem to be linked to pharmaceutical or food manufacturing companies.

With my exercise program already in place and working well, I jumped onto the diabetes pathway. I went 'cold turkey'. The main strategies I set in place within a few days were:

- Eating regular meals with small portions recommended for safe and sustainable weight loss
- Eating every 3-4 hours
- Adding in a wide variety of low glycaemic foods

- Increasing fibre by adding more green leafy and other vegetables

I systematically expanded these strategies with some specifics: I boosted my protein and calcium intake; increased water intake to minimum two litres daily; used only whole grains in small amounts; increased intake of cold water fish (eliminating all other meat); used only low fat dairy; used natural flavourings and sweeteners from herbs, spices and citrus juice; and reduced intake of fat to only olive oil (generally half or less of the amount stated in recipes).

Seven weeks after the commencement of the project, my blood sugar was in the normal range. I had reversed the diabetes.

Ken was very pleased with my progress. But I knew to maintain this success for life, I had to ensure that my workday and personal activities were integrated into a workable schedule that could be sustained.

I had always eaten healthy food—rarely junk food—and enjoyed making delectable entrees to luscious desserts. But I had little thought for how much I ate, or real understanding of the portions that were recommended for health. I was completely ignorant about how to combine different nutrients in foods in a useful way, yet still have delicious and satisfying meals. In short, I ate what I liked. Now, through wide-ranging reading, I understood that it was possible to become obese on good food—when you don't exercise and you eat too much!

The simple equation that I read many times—'more energy out than in'— started to make sense. While I realised that it was a simplification of the process, in order to put it into practice, with a struggling brain, it gave me the basis for planning my day carefully, incorporating the right mix of nutrients, at what time and in conjunction with different types of exercise, regular sleep, timely shopping and meal preparation to make sure that good food was always available.

Above all, a positive mindset was the key to believing in my capacity to make and sustain all the changes during my journey into older age. I could see that this was going to be a challenge at least as tough as recovering from stroke and dealing with cancer.

I began to gain insight into how we live in a world of convenience in all areas of our lives. I had always taken this for granted. But the easy Australian lifestyle, deficient in relevant education that this promotes, is at the expense of our knowledge, our health, our choices and our wallets.

Through the experience of friends I knew that the cost of commercial fad diets was very high. Many of them had experienced the yo-yo cycle of greater weight gain after failing to maintain quick weight loss. Some research showed that pharmaceutical companies, chemists and food manufacturing companies often promote these products accompanied by very expensive nutritional supplements with poor long-term outcomes.

I couldn't understand the peculiar logic of high costs for aggressively advertised so-called healthy diets (particularly just after Christmas and just before spring) that needed the regular and prolonged intake of artificial, expensive supplements or chemical cocktails. I couldn't imagine, even for a day, how unsatisfying it would be to live on food such as 'shakes' or a pill as a nutrient substitute for beautiful fresh food. I could see that this would be unsustainable for me.

I found many websites that claimed to be providing advice on healthy eating. I also saw that there was the risk of information overload, often with confusing half-truths and contradictions. So I focused on research articles written by well-respected experts in Australia and overseas with established reputations whose websites weren't scattered with advertising.

I learned that what I knew about healthy eating was extremely limited. By chance, on one of my trips to the library, I found the *Australian Healthy Food Guide (HFG)* magazine. It provided useful easy-to-read resources for learning about issues such as nutrition, the value of exercise, learning how to read and understand food labels, the hazards of our processed food, our Australian diet and lifestyle issues, and clever and simple recipes.

This was the first Australian resource I had found that was easily accessible, and supported by research, which attempted to simplify the mysteries of healthy living. It frequently mentioned easily-prepared and highly nutritious meals, often using fresh unprocessed ingredients (as close as possible to their natural state), and substantial vegetarian sections that also caught my attention. It seemed logical that unprocessed food—wholefoods—free of preservatives, additives and chemicals with natural levels of sugar, sodium and fat was healthier than our current highly processed diet.

One of the first articles I found, was a list of 'fillers' of high nutrient, low fat, low calorie, and tasty food eaten raw or minimally cooked. This was an excellent tool using readily available and accessible foods to produce healthy meals. I realised that I could make a substantial meal incorporating many of these foods. I set up a subscription to the magazine. *Is this the universe working again?*

I waited eagerly for my first issue in the mail and thoroughly enjoyed reading the articles and recipes as part of my night-time reading. It was a change from wading through complicated research articles, as I began to seriously pursue this part of my journey.

I correlated easier-to-read sources with clinical research where I could, to verify the suggestions from the HFG magazine and various websites.

Fresh Fillers

Vegetables	Vegetables	Fruit
• Artichoke	• Garlic	• Blackberries
• Asparagus	• Green beans	• Blueberries
• Asian greens	• Leek	• Strawberries
• Bean sprouts	• Leafy greens	• Passionfruit
• Bok Choy	• Mushrooms	• Lemon
• Broccoli/broccolini	• Onion	• Lime
• Brussels sprouts	• Parsnip	
• Cabbage	• Radish	
• Chinese cabbage	• Silver beet	
• Capsicum	• Snow peas	
• Carrot	• Spinach	
• Cauliflower	• Sugar snap peas	
• Celeriac	• Tomato	
• Celery	• Turnip	
• Cucumber	• Watercress	
• Eggplant	• Zucchini	
• Fennel		

Courtesy of the *Australian Healthy Food Guide* magazine

As I delved further into this area, I wanted to know how and how much I was eating, and what balance of nutrients was required to offset exercise. There was a mountain of information available, although at times it was overwhelming and confusing. Many foods recommended even by many dietitians, had significant levels of added sugar, salt and fat. The meal plan produced by the Diabetes Council in the information given to me when I had been diagnosed with diabetes, suggested eating mostly commercially processed food—just less of it. Even with my limited knowledge this didn't seem to add up, when there were better and healthier wholefood alternatives.

I also found that the correct size portions recommended by authoritative nutritionists and dietitians, rarely aligned with recipe servings given in popular recipe websites.

With little effort I quickly discovered that using unprocessed foods opened a whole new world of accessible, affordable, easily prepared, digestible and highly nutritious food. I found small portions eaten slowly were delicious and filling.

I became conscious of the dubious nature of our food labelling. Where possible, I avoided products that said 'made from local and imported ingredients' even among unprocessed foods. However, some foods such as dates—fresh or dried—are simply not readily grown and sold in Australia. Although we produce them in Alice Springs, the industry is in its infancy and the produce is not easily obtained. Reading the labels on imported dates I saw that some contained palm oil (often written as vegetable oil). I immediately began to soak and rinse (twice) commercial dried dates with boiling water to remove the palm oil used as a preservative, before turning them into date puree for recipes that required some sweetening.

I remembered the kilometres of orchards on the Central Coast of NSW that I saw as a child. They produced beautiful stone fruits such as apricots. Now long gone, we are forced to buy mostly imported dried apricots. However, with little effort I thoroughly enjoyed dehydrating them in season, grown in Australia, to provide my own delicious dried fruit and fruit leathers. I also learned that by reconstituting a small amount of my own dried fruit with the addition only of chia seed to make the right consistency, in five minutes I could process them into delicious jam for buckwheat toast.

As I plunged headlong into my research, I realised how I had missed out for so many years on the taste of natural foods. Like most people, I had become accustomed to the idea that the best food needed sugar, fat and salt to make it palatable. By changing my shopping mindset, I found that there was an abundance of locally produced fresh food, available close to home. As I built my gourmet pantry staples on these foods, this drastically lowered my overall food bills. I found that I could easily afford to buy fresh, locally grown and mainly Australian produce, and help our farmers along the way.

For example, I realised that by paying $5 for a kilo of Australian dried chickpeas, I had many home-made meals and options available. With some cooked and frozen always ready for use (it takes the same time to cook ¼ cup as two cups), I easily learned to work with this magical legume to provide different tastes and textures: cooked as a base for soups and casseroles, ground into flour, rolled in zesty herbs and spices and roasted as snacks, processed for hummus, added to salads, curries, dips or recipes for many different meals and cuisines. This meant avoiding paying for gloopy water with salt, additives and preservatives in the canned variety. Only ¼ cup of dried chickpeas is enough to make low-cost chickpea, carrot and sweet potato soup for 6-8 servings: nutrient-dense, satisfying and delicious: enough for a meal or two and some for the freezer. A kilo is a lot of dried chickpeas!

I learned to work with many other unprocessed foods in this way. By gradually building up my pantry stocks I had ample staples to give me highly varied, readily available food. With planning and thinking differently about when and how to prepare food, I easily found lists of affordable seasonal produce to keep me healthy and interested in wholefoods.

This pathway also took me to websites, research and blogs written by extraordinary and creative, well-known (and some not-so-well known) chefs, farmers, cooks and ordinary people with an interest in healthy eating. They knew how to maximise their enjoyment of food, with higher nutrition and at a fraction of the cost of conventional and highly processed convenience foods. I didn't need to develop my own recipes as I found them in abundance online.

After a lifetime of a typical Australian diet, and all that it encompassed in convenience of purchasing, availability and preparation, it necessitated a complete change of mindset to make this enormous conversion sustainable. I realised that for success in regaining good health as quickly as possible, I had to follow this pathway meticulously. It couldn't be a half-and-half eating plan.

The quick results even in the early stages, gave me the impetus to continue exploring this unknown world. In the following weeks and months, I refined, streamlined, tested and re-organised my shopping, eating patterns and kitchen routines till they became my daily practice. I virtually eliminated my use of additives, preservatives and hidden sugar, fat and salt. I was surprised at how quickly and easily this could be accomplished. I felt healthier, happier, and more energetic.

I saw this new way of eating as an integration challenge, incorporating many small programs to educate myself on completely unfamiliar ideas and concepts to form 'the big picture'. I gained a sense of achievement in benefitting my recovery of all three illnesses: reversing diabetes through improved health, boosting my well-being to minimise the likelihood of the cancer returning, and re-building my brain's capacity in restoring my language. It gave my self-confidence a boost as everything began to fall into place.

On any weekday, when I needed to integrate my work with other tasks in my kitchen, this meant improving my planning skills. For example: taking a few minutes in the morning before work to mix delicious, homemade and healthy buckwheat bread, leaving it for a few hours while it looked after itself, completing other tasks on my work schedule with associated WBAs, then cooking it quickly as part of a delicious lunch. This had great value for my recovering brain by having to link tasks over lengthier periods and remember where I was up to in order to complete the activity in a timely manner.

My kitchen became an environment of exciting programs. The tangible reward was the rich aroma of foods such as roasting almonds to be turned quickly into homemade almond butter, slow-cooking braised red cabbage with apple, easily-made nutritious black bean soup with fresh-baked bread and delicious salads. This led to less cooking, and reduced my use of electricity, water and time spent in cleaning up.

What I thought initially might be an expensive way of purchasing food, now revealed itself to be very cheap, easy to prepare—and definitely gourmet!

As I learned more about the importance of regularising food intake with activity to maintain optimum blood sugar, my list of WBAs grew quickly and now had many more interesting entries. I looked for ways that I could maximise the availability of WBAs. I followed each meal with a minimum of 20 minutes of activity, from my early morning walk to walking around the block after lunch or dinner, to making vigorous WBAs into exercises in the afternoon, using them to improve my mobility and flexibility and implementing them regularly across each day.

With each discovery about using unprocessed foods, I could also see the pressure of aggressive marketing to purchase more efficient appliances often with very hefty price tags. But I learned that many genuine users of unprocessed foods use very ordinary kitchen implements. I discovered that the simplicity and joy of preparing these foods didn't need a kitchen of high-tech space-consuming gadgets.

Alana's Gourmet Pantry

- Using seasonal, fresh and unprocessed/whole foods where possible.
- Growing major staples such as many green leafy vegetables, sprouts, tomatoes, eggplant, sweet potato, rhubarb, berries, and oranges.
- Making fermented and preserved foods, dressings, spreads and breads.
- Grinding herbs, seeds and spices.

Herbs:	• Parsley, chives, rosemary, coriander, mint, thyme, smoked paprika, cumin, caraway seeds, fennel seeds, oregano, thyme, dill, tarragon, turmeric, chilli, garlic, ginger and others
Dairy:	• Cheese: parmesan, low fat feta, ricotta and cottage • Yogurt: home made with skim milk and commercial starter • Milk: Skim milk (dairy) and home-made almond milk
Fats/Oil:	• Olive oil • Macadamia or sesame oil (occasionally)
Spreads:	• Hummus: original, beetroot or roasted red capsicum • Fresh fruit jam with chia • Nut and peanut butters • No margarine or butter of any kind

Nuts/seeds:	• Almonds, walnuts and peanuts (natural in their shells) • Pecans, macadamias, hazel and pistachios • Chia, flax, pepitas, pinenuts, sunflower, poppy, nigella, sesame
Spices:	• Nutmeg, ground cinnamon, ginger, cardamom, cloves, allspice • Homemade combinations of Middle Eastern, Indian, Italian and other mixes for tagines and curries
Legumes:	• Peas (yellow/green), chickpeas (yellow/brown), barley, beans (kidney, cannellini, butter, white, black, broad, borlotti, black-eyed). • Lentils (green, orange, brown, puy)
Sprouts:	• Mung beans, lentils, broccoli, alfalfa, radish, buckwheat, kale
Fish:	• Canned salmon, sardines, kippers • Other fish as available, sustainably caught, local and fresh
Meat:	• No beef, lamb, pork or chicken (due to poor animal welfare legislation)

Vegetables: (Home-grown or purchased fresh and unbagged)	• Lettuce, baby spinach, silver beet, pak choy, cabbage (several types), rocket, celery, cavalero nero, celery, broccoli/broccolini, cauliflower • Shallot, red/brown onion, leek • Sweet potato, carrot, potato, beetroot • Tomatoes • Mushrooms • Capsicum, eggplant, zucchini, cucumber, olives • Pumpkin
Eggs:	• Always 2-3 hard-boiled eggs in the fridge • Home-made whole egg mayonnaise (occasionally)
Soup: (Home-made)	• Several varieties in the freezer at all times
Grains:	• Oats, rye, quinoa, couscous, polenta, wheat including freekeh. • Wholemeal lasagne and pasta (occasionally) • Rice (brown or basmati) • Flours: rye, buckwheat, wheat, chickpea
Fruits:	• Apple, orange, banana (most days) • Strawberries, blueberries, raspberries • Grapes • Rhubarb • Peaches, nectarines, plums • Cranberries (occasionally) • Mango (occasionally)

Bread & Muffins: (Home-made)	• Various hand-made gluten and non-gluten breads and various yeast/no yeast breads (no commercial bread mixes) • Muffins made with wholemeal flours or almond meal
Preserved & Fermented Food: (Home-made)	• Preserved lemons • Marinated red capsicum, cucumber, chargrilled eggplant • Sauerkraut • Kimchi • Pickles
Dressings:	• Fresh squeezed lemon, orange, lime juices • Olive oil • Balsamic, white/red wine vinegar • Seeded mustard, dijon mustard (home-made) • Sweet/smoked paprika • Yogurt-based 'mayonnaise' mixed with some fresh herbs
Dehydrated Food:	• Tomatoes, zucchini, eggplant • Lemons, oranges, strawberries, kiwi fruit • Ginger and turmeric (home-grown)
Drinks	• Up to 2.5 litres per day • Coffee mostly decaf • Decaf green tea • Fresh orange and mint, lemongrass and ginger teas

Sweeteners:	• Cinnamon
	• Nutmeg
	• Fresh/dried dates for puree (palm oil preservative removed)
	• Dried apricots, sultanas, raisins and prunes
	• Honey (rarely)
	• Carob (rarely)
	• Cocoa (rarely)
Extras:	• Ryvita biscuits
	• No commercial desserts, or processed meals of any kind
	• No takeaway food of any kind
	• Grilled fish or vegetarian dish at restaurants
	• Anchovies for flavouring and for making salsa verde (occasionally)
Desserts:	• Ice cream on special occasions.

… and, I didn't cheat! From day 1 of the project, I stayed with my plan.

I also realised that to purchase expensive appliances had more than financial costs—it meant taking away the joy and satisfaction of producing beautiful and nutritious food in ways that most of us had forgotten or never learned to do. It also meant missing out on the tactile satisfaction and fulfilment of nurturing, manipulating and integrating ingredients that combine wonderful flavours, colours and textures. I found sufficient (sometimes forgotten) tools that I already had in my kitchen and put them to use.

To make sure that my seven-week diabetes reversal hadn't been achieved by chance, I looked more widely in optimising my health. Many people have remarked that my achievement was the result of "just changing diet and exercise". While these were undoubtedly important factors, over time I retrained myself out of a lifetime of behaviours and habits to maintain the reversal.

My success was the result of a change in mindset in many lifestyle factors and priorities: good nutrition including substantial water intake; exercise linked directly to food intake and type; planning, prioritising and scheduling daily activities; managing stress and anxiety; relaxation; and regular and adequate sleep. Some of these were non-negotiable and to my surprise they easily slotted into my new schedules. It was a function of intensive self-education, perseverance, being assertive when faced with challenges and questioning and challenging outdated ideas from some HPs and associated services.

"Once you're diagnosed with diabetes you've got it for life", is a pervasive statement in our literature and frequently stated by HPs. It is easy to proceed on this negative pathway and fall into the trap of learned helplessness. It takes curiosity, creativity as an individual, commitment to self-education and sustainable behaviour change. While not every one can, or wants to, reverse this condition, it is clearly achievable for many people when they become aware of its possibility.

*

I was on a roll. I constantly reviewed my strategies to maintain the momentum of recovery across the three illnesses, making changes where necessary. I decided to widen the use of music from relaxation to recovering my skills in linking information, anticipating, planning and maintaining concentration.

Music was a free, readily available resource. I began to use it as a tool for re-training my brain to connect information, by practising linking sections of a lengthy piece of music. I had experienced the frustration of faltering in smoothly linking passages of music that had previously been familiar, such as when playing the 'Hallelujah

Chorus' for the choirs or even simple songs with several sections such as 'We've Done Us Proud'. I had played this music for many years. Now I often lost concentration and couldn't anticipate the next section in my mind. Subsequently, I often missed some of the fine detail of rhythm and technique in intricate sections. This increased my frustration—and my blood pressure.

This motivated me to go back to my earliest ways of practising classical music as a young student: breaking down the bar or section, practising it slowly, getting it right before moving on to the next bar or section, linking those that I had learned, practising them as whole sections then gradually linking the whole piece. It was frustrating, tedious, and sometimes note-by-note across many practice sessions.

However, each time I achieved even a small improvement I congratulated myself on my success. So I began to look for the small gains, especially on those days when I was fatigued or had what I called a 'down day'. I also reminded myself that because I had learned it once, it was easier the second time around.

While I was renowned for turning up to choir practice with only a few minutes to spare after a rushed trip, I scheduled myself to leave home earlier, and used the extra time in a leisurely drive to practise memory recall and concentration. I set myself tasks such as remembering the names of different types of songs in our repertoire, recalling our first and last songs the previous week, thinking of song titles from the evening's list of around 30 songs, special requests and new songs that we were learning. I thought through those that I had struggled with, and set those as tasks at home in my music-based WBAs. Initially, I could rarely remember the answers to these questions. These exercises slowly re-acquainted me with our repertoire and continued to rebuild my confidence.

At choir rehearsals we experimented with the placement of the piano, so the direction of sound coming from the piano didn't 'clash' with the singing, causing me to hear confused and unintelligible noise. Placed strategically, my brain didn't have to struggle as hard to differentiate the sound of the piano from the voices. This was another gain in reducing the barriers raised by the auditory processing disorder in a noisy environment.

Over those early weeks after returning to choir rehearsal, my brain began to adjust to the sound in the room. I dared to hope that I was slowly improving from this debilitating and frustrating disorder. However, I was reminded of its impact when on one occasion the choir sang 'Those Magnificent Men in their Flying Machines', a light-hearted, fun song in which one of our choristers plays a high pitched whistle to simulate the sound of a whizzing spitfire plane. I had heard the whistle many times during rehearsals and performances over the years. But this time the sound was so piercing I could hardly bear it. I read later that the fractured brain may overcompensate for loss of auditory processing and be unable to 'regulate' loud or high-pitched sound. There were several similar experiences, including a child screaming loudly in a restaurant, that I found disproportionately deafening. Over several months my brain slowly adjusted to this phenomenon until it was functioning at a comfortable level.

With continuous auditory exercises, my memory began to improve as my auditory processing strengthened. I could differentiate words, voices and conversations more easily.

To many people it seemed that my hearing was affected. It was easier to agree, than try to explain the complex nature of an auditory processing disorder. The singers accepted my difficulty without judgment, kept up their encouragement, treated me like one of the group, and kept singing (like all good performers) regardless of what I played. We laughed when Annette announced a song but I began to play something entirely different.

> *Diary entry after a choir rehearsal:*
> A tenor requested that the choir sing 'All My
> Loving', for his birthday request.
> My brain heard: 'All You Need is Love.'
> (Sometimes my brain tried to help out by filling in
> the black holes, but didn't always succeed!)

ABC Radio also became an important resource. On Classic FM I saturated myself with classical music at home and often while driving. I practised differentiating violins, woodwinds, brass, percussion or other instruments. To help in building my skills in sequencing numbers I counted single beats and bars then multiples of bars of music for as long as I could before I lost concentration. With long pieces, I could practise many sequences. I found that over time, I became better at counting accurately for longer periods with less loss of concentration. I listened to different musical genres such as swing and traditional through to extreme jazz, which really challenged my concentration in counting (Dave Brubeck's 'Take 5' was a quirky tool!).

I also listened to radio stations playing easy listening music, so I could practise regaining my articulation through singing. Initially, this was very difficult as there was either no introduction to the song by the radio presenter or I couldn't follow their words because of the auditory processing disorder. Singing was very challenging as the words and phrases were sung in time with the rhythm of the music, but not necessarily that of normal conversation. This meant expressing words in different ways and changing the rhythm of my language to match the beat. On many occasions, I struggled with remembering the name and words of songs that I had known for years. As I generally didn't know which music would be played next, I had to be very alert.

I tried singing in harmony to simple sequences of notes played on the piano. As a professional musician I was accomplished in this skill and I was proficient in harmonising spontaneously with melodies and singers. But now I failed, realising that it was too early in my recovery to succeed in such a complex task—playing one melody while singing and improvising in another. I shelved this skill to a later time.

To increase the challenge I listened to the iPod while gardening in my front yard, to simulate more spontaneous sounds from different sources near the road. This had wider application in rebuilding my independence in safety with a high level of competing environmental noise, e.g. when the sound came from behind me, such as a car on the road or a friend who greeted me from behind in a supermarket.

During the cricket season I used Jim Maxwell's commentary on ABC Radio to listen for phrasing and rhythm from his voice, then repeated his phrases as drill. His pronunciation and varying speed of speech was an excellent tool as he commented on the Test matches. I listened to his voice carefully during explanation, questioning, humour, rhetorical questions, emphasis, phrasing and rhythm. This was particularly demanding as I had no visual cues and no knowledge of cricket. I also used newsreaders and weather presenters on television to practise recognising different individual language patterns (I tried watching soaps, but they were too slow!). I noticed significant differences between articulation of presenters that I had not noticed prior to the stroke. Vanessa O'Hanlon, the National Weather Presenter on ABC 24 News Breakfast, provided an excellent role model for me to practise articulation and rhythm with her melodic and easy style of communication.

When walking past a group of local school students during my morning walk I often concentrated on identifying different types of voices, the pace and emotion of the conversation (fast/slow and happy/sad), listened for the rhythm of the voice and tried to identify some key words within 2-3 seconds of passing them.

After reading about the implications of an auditory processing disorder, on one night I set my mobile phone alarm for 2.30am in an adjoining room. The purpose was to see if my brain could wake me from deep sleep in the event of an alert such as a smoke alarm. I was very relieved when it worked.

Mastering these exercises took extensive rebuilding of my skills in sound differentiation and concentration, but I grasped any opportunity at anytime during the day or night. I could recognise that my skills were gradually improving—even accelerating in the rebound into normal language.

Chapter Eight

Project Review: Picking Up the Pace

Several events occurred in quick succession that led me to rethink my plan:

1. Conversation with Rod (local vet): I visited him to renew medications for my frail, elderly dogs. He was shocked to hear of my health issues. As I left, he remarked, "There must have been something to trigger all three illnesses at once. What was it? Were you working too hard?" I quickly explained that my weight had been the problem. But as I drove home I wondered at his comment. Working hard was expected in small business and I had always taken on this challenge with great enthusiasm, never seeing the stress involved as detrimental to my health.

2. Meeting with Ken: although he was very supportive of my recovery efforts, he now cautioned me about becoming stressed prior to my upcoming cancer surgery because of the risk to my blood pressure. He was well aware that I could become anxious when discussing some of my experiences in hospital, and he urged me to take care to stay calm. For a second time in a few days the issue of stress had been raised.

3. Phone call from Heather: she suggested that we try weekly tai chi classes as a way of non-impact exercise, reduction of stress and a form of relaxation. I enjoyed the classes, and within a few weeks I had started a range of exercises before getting out of bed—tai chi speed—beginning with finger and toe joints and gradually working through major joints and muscles. Within a short time this enabled me to step out of bed with no joint stiffness, muscle soreness or

fasciitis and to move around with my limbs and muscles already warmed up, ready for the day.

4. Another idea from Heather: always pragmatic, she suggested attending a local seminar conducted by a local Buddhist group entitled, 'Why Worry'. She suggested that it could be one way of learning how to meditate for relaxation, reduce stress and lower blood pressure. I happily agreed to attend the seminar and learn what I could. I found the principles interesting, so I attended a follow-up seminar a week later that reinforced the ideas. During this session, a woman asked the seminar leader about a problem she had been experiencing with a teenager, resulting in extreme stress. He carefully explained, "Sometimes in dealing with a problem, we become stressed because we focus on the wrong goal."

As I walked out of the seminar, I was suddenly struck by the realisation that I had set the wrong pathways for my project. I saw that they were fragmented, fragile, restrictive—even unachievable. In my desperation to achieve an optimum level of recovery and health but with an impaired ability to conceptualise the big picture, I had fallen into the trap of setting elusive targets.

With my hard work, I had achieved significant gains in a relatively short time and maintained the momentum of what had become a very busy life. However, I had inadvertently set myself up for increasing my level of stress—possibly raising my blood pressure to dangerous levels, triggering recurrence of cancer, returning to old eating habits then potentially returning to a diabetic state.

Like most people, I used the term 'stress' in an off-handed way. I realised that I needed to explore it further, understand it better, and prevent it occurring to an abnormal level.

I began wading through information in the ocean of available articles to educate myself on 'what it is,' 'when it happens', 'its triggers' and 'its prevention'. I learned enough in a short period of time to realise that it's insidious, often unrecognised in the frantic nature of our daily lives, and potentially destructive in its outcomes. The accumulation of many instances of stress leading to continual hypertension highlighted how it had become too easy for our society to treat stress with medication as the treatment of choice, rather than deal with the cause. I now realised that it had been one of the significant factors that had led to my catastrophic ill-health. This realisation was like the final piece in the jigsaw.

It was a light globe moment! With my improving skills in analysing information and applying new knowledge, I realised that I was focused on preventing illness, rather than improving wellness—a much broader, positive, functional concept. *Is this an indication that I am rebuilding my higher order thinking skills?*

The concept of developing strategies that are based on flexibility and lateral thinking was more manageable. This was more likely to yield realistic and positive outcomes, given the unpredictable nature of life.

*

During my reading on recovery from illness, I had occasionally come across the phrase, 'change your lifestyle'. With only a vague understanding of what this phrase really meant, and no comprehension of the enormity of its implications, it hadn't featured as part of my thinking. I hadn't specifically researched 'change of lifestyle' in all of my reading. But now, when I did, there were many references tied to stroke, cancer and diabetes that mentioned change of lifestyle. *But what does it mean?* I found that aside from vague statements there was little detail on the process. *How do I actually change my lifestyle?*

Paradoxically, I had already begun the process of complete lifestyle change in integrating my actions to deal with three illnesses simultaneously—but I hadn't recognised or labelled it as such. Because my strategies had targeted the illnesses, I was not focusing on the real health outcomes that I needed, and wanted, in the long term—a changed lifestyle.

I laughed when I read some of the websites offering tips for changing your lifestyle. Like much of the education on dealing with major illnesses I had read, it didn't go far enough. With even my limited but growing knowledge, I realised that it generally focused on one or two specific aspects of lifestyle. It didn't highlight (or rarely mentioned), how changing one aspect of life had implications for every other part of one's life, in every minute of every day.

The term 'lifestyle change' has become a nice-sounding and convenient marketing term. In reality, it is meaningless and unachievable when dealt with in a disjointed way. When linked with the fear of a serious illness such as stroke, cancer or diabetes, the marketing often suggests that changing behaviour, such as weight loss of 5kg, is sufficient to change the lifestyle that has led to the problem. In the face of aggressive marketing and fragmented education about lifestyle issues relating to eating, aging, weight loss, work/life balance, sleep, retirement, well-being and recreation, one could be easily persuaded into believing that changing any one of those life areas is all you need to do—tagged with significant cost. The 'fear factor' has become very powerful in convincing consumers to part with many dollars in the elusive and mysterious quest for success.

Yet it is widely reported in research, and in the media, that there is a tendency for the majority of people to revert to poor habits after initial success. This often leads to more negative outcomes. I realised, that to achieve sustained behaviour change—real and comprehensive lifestyle change—*everything* in my life had to change. One action would impact many others, which in turn would also need to change.

It felt like moving to a foreign country where I had to quickly learn how to survive independently in a new and unfamiliar culture. It relied on education followed by relevant action in my daily behaviours. This was the key, so that they became sustainable routines. I had to be conscious of what I did in my teachable moments, and realise that everything in my lifestyle was linked.

Recognising the 'ripple effect' became relevant to my project, in which I explored how far the ripples extended when learning a new skill or an unfamiliar topic. This tested my capacity to think at a much higher level. From separate negative illness-focused targets, I now moved to my project *strategy*, which became:

> 'Optimise survival through continuous lifestyle change.'

Putting the right strategy in place meant that I had achieved a significant project milestone that enabled the journey to turn a corner, and accelerate with a kick!

Suddenly, as the fog began to dissipate more quickly, I could see the world in a different way. I was reminded that Adele had begun her support with talking about the journey. She had once said to me that I would one day see the stroke as a "stroke of luck", and that this journey was the catalyst that I needed to realign my priorities. Understanding what it really meant to change one's lifestyle was the ticket for the journey to survival.

I realised that anyone's lifestyle is impossible to prescribe. How do you change a lifetime of behaviours—ASAP—for life? Perhaps this was why the education or detail on how to do this was relatively sparse, and couched in indefinable goals and vague, convoluted language. How can one person prescribe how to change someone else's lifestyle beyond whimsical, vague statements? It seemed that while some writers promoted its value, they had clearly not engaged in the process. I could see that suggestions of "losing 5kg" or "changing your job" or "increasing exercise", on their own, harboured the tools of failure.

The excitement of my new focus on strategies was that they could be whatever I wanted them to be, while I remained unconstrained by society's expectations of the life stages. There were realistic and practical opportunities there for the taking. For me, the saying, "Make the best of every day", became "Make the best <u>of every</u>

<u>minute</u> of every day", for life. This fitted with my teachable moments concept that now became heightened in practical reality. This didn't mean that I had to be doing 'something' at all times, but it meant being continually *aware* of everything I did, reflecting on the value of the activity, maximising its benefit and where possible, doing it better next time around, just like engineers. I had to think of my recovering brain as working in 'manual' rather than 'automatic' to take advantage of each opportunity. *Be conscious of what I'm doing at all times.* I became vigilant in looking for opportunities for learning, re-learning and extending my skills in all that I did.

*

Cancer surgery was imminent. Armed with a new enthusiasm and motivation, I turned to practising the techniques I had recently learned on meditation and reducing anxiety, to deal with my apprehension during the days leading up to the event. My greatest fear was that I might have another stroke during the surgery. There were times when it was difficult to stay positive. I made sure that in each day, at least one or two WBAs were devoted to a few minutes of meditation to assist in reducing the potential for raising my stress. I could measure that, and know if it was working, with a very simple machine.

Being appreciative of the value and comfort of good friends, I relied heavily on Heather, Annette and Adele to talk with and listen to me through my concerns in person, via email or Skype. While I sometimes bombarded them with my thoughts, I realised that my emails were now coherent with rare errors.

A few days before cancer surgery, I attended a pre-operative meeting with Georgia, the Anaesthetist. I was under no illusions about my heightened risk of another stroke by undergoing anaesthetic. I was reassured by her friendly and down-to-earth manner as she talked about how the surgery would occur. I begged her to let me die if I suffered another stroke during the surgery. While I knew this was beyond her capability, the likely outcome of waking with a second stroke was more than I could contemplate. I was desperate. I didn't know how I could will myself to die if this scenario occurred, without help. While I was still fearful as I left the meeting, I felt assured that she would do her very best to avoid this outcome.

I woke feeling apprehensive on the day planned for the surgery. When thinking about the statistics I had read on survival and recurrence of cancer, I reminded myself of David's frank and honest responses to my questions. He had emphasised the positive outcomes for the majority of women treated for breast cancer, especially when it was diagnosed at an early stage. It was easy to feel hopeful when talking to him.

I had proceeded through all aspects of the pre-operative planning, feeling confident in David's expertise and my chances of a positive result. But now that the day—the moment—had arrived, I was confronted by the situation in which the surgery had to be done to increase my chances of survival. But this remedy was, in itself, a possible catalyst for a worst-case scenario. The fear of another stroke—an unwanted potential complication of surgery that had always been at the back of my mind—was now at the forefront of my thoughts.

I felt comforted by seeing Georgia in the Anaesthetic Bay. My recollection as the anaesthetic began to take effect was that she said:

"Do you have any other questions?"
"Please bring me back without another stroke".

As I woke slowly from the anaesthetic—the blackness that feels like you have lost part of your life—and realising that the surgery was over, I cautiously wriggled my fingers and toes and found there was no paralysis. When David spoke to me as I was preparing to leave Recovery, I was more interested in this outcome than whether or not the surgery had been successful:

"No stroke?" I asked.

"No stroke." he replied.

I was grateful for his expertise and hadn't doubted his success in removing the tumour. The results were positive with no evidence of spread of the cancer. As I recovered during the next few weeks, I was grateful for his wise counsel to opt for "Lumpectomy, then let's wait and see."

The next steps were radiation and hormone therapy. While this entailed working with different areas of cancer services, there were commonalities that I noticed from the outset that were not apparent in stroke services. My questions were welcomed and I was part of the decision-making. I had many questions. During interactions with the HPs they showed that they were courteous, patient and respectful.

When on one occasion another member of the medical team made a decision that could have derailed the recovery plan that David and I had negotiated, he acted swiftly and decisively to keep things on track. I appreciated his leadership and was satisfied that I was in good hands for overcoming this illness. I felt ready to face the radiation therapy in the following weeks.

While I was mindful that recurrence of cancer was a possibility, at no time did I feel that there was no hope, or that I couldn't make a substantial effort to help myself to survive this disease. This thread of hope underpinned the literature, anecdotes, blogs, books and support groups for people experiencing breast cancer that I read constantly, prior to and after the surgery. I was determined to become as educated as I could, given my difficulty in comprehending unfamiliar information. In the health services that I attended during this part of my journey, I could see that from hospital assistants and administrative staff, through to nursing staff, radiation therapists, and surgical and medical staff such as David and André, there was obvious commitment to doing their very best for their patients.

*

Shortly after cancer surgery, I returned to daytime performances with the choirs. I was apprehensive about my first gig, held at a nursing home.

Although my auditory processing disorder had improved in the rehearsal rooms, it was untested at a gig. At venues with large performance spaces such as nursing homes, halls and clubs, unmoveable pianos were often placed behind the singers or to the side of the performance area with my back to them and the conductor. There was always a high level of echo and other incidental environmental noise. It was almost impossible for me to understand what was said by the conductor to the audience as an introduction to each song. So I learned to listen to the rise and fall of their voice without understanding their words, and wait for a slight pause as they turned back to the choir. Then I listened for, "OK Alana". My brain could understand those words. This was the signal to start playing.

This became a good exercise for concentration in listening to pattern, rhythm, intonation, and pausing in speech. With Annette, John and Lorraine as conductors, this became my strategy to ensure that our singers could perform at their best with timely accompaniment. On some occasions, when the piano was buried completely behind the group, a singer in the back row let me know when to start. This teamwork and sense of unconditional acceptance of my difficulties embodied the philosophy of the singers. This motivated me to persevere in continuing to reduce the auditory processing difficulty in various contexts. To my relief, with my confidence slowly returning, I was also recognising its steady improvement.

*

During this time, I also intensified my exercise schedule. I changed my Sunday morning relaxation walk (purposeful pace) around my local community, to a long walk to an unfamiliar destination. I wanted to work on building my stamina and endurance. I thoroughly enjoyed this addition to my program. I felt pleased with myself that I was confident in being away from the safety of home for a lengthy period.

But even on a quiet Sunday walk, the auditory processing difficulty needed careful management.

One morning, after heavy overnight rain, I was dodging some large puddles on the path at the lake. As I stepped to the right, a cyclist quickly swerved onto the grass to avoid me and made some very disparaging remarks (that I was glad I couldn't understand), as she came to a stop.

"Where's your bell?"
"I rang it, twice! Are you deaf?" She glared at me,
as she hopped back onto her bike.
"It's complicated!" I shouted as she rode away.

This was not the time to explain the mysteries of an auditory processing disorder to an angry stranger. While this incident reminded me of the hazards of interacting in the community away from my comfort zone, it also reminded me that by observing some simple rules I could markedly reduce the risk. From then on, I always walked to the left and looked behind me, before moving to the other side of the path.

My Sunday walks often lasted for up to four hours. Anywhere. My Health Data Sheet records that over several months, I walked at 15 different locations, many that I had never visited before on foot. This meant I was now spending around 16 hours each week, walking a minimum of 10,000 steps each day and up to 20,000 steps on a Sunday, complemented by additional daily exercise through WBAs.

When shopping, I had established regular behaviours such as mostly buying those items that I could carry back to the car without a trolley. This gave me incidental exercise in carrying weights and posture practice as I routinely parked the furthest distance from the supermarket. Ironically, my loads of items became less over time, as I shopped mostly just to keep the pantry stocked, with an evolving list of favourite foods and staples. I was thoroughly enjoying my new gourmet food, feeling healthier, more energetic, and with a renewed positive outlook on my chances of survival.

On three days over several months when it was too wet to walk, I drove to a large shopping centre and briskly walked around for almost two hours to keep up my step count. I felt good that I had good self-discipline in resisting the tempting aromas from bakeries or cafés. I also politely refused the offer of coffee and cakes at the conclusion of gigs. If I felt tempted I asked myself whether the short-term gratification was worth the risk to my long-term lasting benefit in better quality of life. This was enough for me to keep walking past the café and just drink tea or water at gigs. I didn't cheat or deviate from my plan at any time in my new exercise and eating routines.

Social events were also a chance to practise my auditory processing during the jovial conversation among the singers that always followed a gig. I retrained my brain to concentrate on listening and responding to light-hearted banter. My ability to recognise the subtleties of humour in conversation was improving. I knew that my brain was adapting to following different voice tones, speed of speech and conversations. In the relaxed atmosphere with friends, I felt less afraid of stumbling and I noticed that my black holes were becoming much less frequent.

*

In preparation for radiation therapy several weeks after the cancer surgery I read extensively on healthy eating and activity when undergoing this treatment. I followed the advice meticulously. The tumour had been comprised mostly of oestrogen, so I avoided any foods or chemicals that could increase my oestrogen levels. This was easy with my use of whole foods. My gourmet pantry of almost all fresh and unprocessed food meant that everything I ate had high nutrient value. I was feeling the benefit in my skin, nails, hair, digestive health and feeling of well-being.

Heather and I often talked about the chemical additives and preservatives in our food. We agreed that our own vegetable garden was a good idea. She set one up at home, and after only two hours one Sunday afternoon, we had set up a small vegetable garden for me, modelled on the No Dig Garden method—easy to manage and great fun!

As a novice gardener I knew very little, but with regular chats with Heather, the help of a gardening app on my iPad, and some trial and error, I grew some beautiful vegetables and herbs in my first growing season. They were tasty, Australian grown, seasonal, fresh, accessible at any time, and pesticide-free. I covered my delicious tomatoes with old sheer white curtains to prevent destruction by fruit fly. I called them my 'brides in the garden'. I experienced the exquisite taste of strawberries picked for breakfast, ripe tomatoes full of flavour and fresh leafy greens harvested for a crisp, delicious salad at lunch. I included something from my garden in every meal.

I was very excited about the new interests in my life and spent a few minutes in the garden every morning after my walk. I happily shared my strawberries with the little birds or other creatures that came into the garden. I felt very proud as my spinach, tomatoes, rhubarb, eggplant, sweet potatoes and herbs turned into beautiful produce for eating raw, cooking, dehydrating, pickling and freezing.

*

My work pace was regaining momentum. By this stage, I had completed 11 sessions of three-hour interview training programs for clients from very different backgrounds including Skype training with some long distance clients. This training was always intensive, and although I still rehearsed more than I had ever done in previous years to ensure the integrity of the training, I knew that my skills were returning more quickly in successfully planning and adapting the training to suit client's individual needs. I could feel my confidence returning with the training falling smoothly into place, from separate sections into an integrated, logical and functional education program.

With stroke recovery well-advanced, diabetes reversed and tumour removed, whatever challenges the radiation treatment would bring, I was ready to face them with optimism.

On the first day of radiation therapy I was a little apprehensive, but reassured by the professional and friendly approach by everyone involved in the service. I felt that I had an army of support behind me.

As a breast cancer patient I could appreciate the value of the powerful marketing message underpinning their philosophy, and promoted across the community: hope, respect, support and well-being—so necessary to battle this disease. Clever and consistent media marketing associates breast cancer with 'pink and beautiful'. Far from trivialising breast cancer, I felt buoyed by the positive images of people everywhere, living normal lives. I was very grateful to be a beneficiary of this approach.

During my radiation treatment program over 25 days, I also saw opportunities to integrate my auditory processing practice. The service was very busy and the therapists were efficient and highly organised. They rarely kept me waiting for more than a few minutes. I used those few minutes in the waiting room to practise listening for my name being called, while concentrating on reading a book. There was a myriad of distracting sounds in the area. As the radiation therapists were different each day, my brain wasn't familiar with their voices. I felt good that my practice at home in recognising spontaneous sounds while multi-tasking simple activities, were being applied successfully in another teachable moment in a different context.

A further opportunity arose when being positioned on the treatment table, where, I was unable to see the faces of the radiation therapists. I used these few minutes to ask simple questions about radiation therapy, without interrupting their work. To hear their responses, I had to concentrate on listening and understanding the response without visual cues.

When the therapists left the room during the treatment, I practised counting the seconds between closing the door until when the machine began its cycle. Even for a few seconds, this was a chance to concentrate, practising counting in succession and later asking a question about why the time varied or some other aspect of radiation treatment. The therapists were amused when I later told them how I was undertaking two therapy sessions—one for the stroke, and one for the cancer. But even in these transient moments, I had to discipline myself to suppress the surreal and off-putting sense of feeling like a piece of meat from the neck up while speaking and counting, and like a goddess from the neck down, while being gently positioned by the radiation therapists.

In some reflective moments, I wondered how it could be that two health services in a modern country like Australia could be so different. There was nothing less dangerous or less ugly about breast cancer—but the approach to its management was clearly different to that of stroke. For breast cancer it was about optimism regarding recovery, engagement with the patient to the level at which they desired, and creating a positive environment to lift a patient's hope and motivation. For stroke services, it felt like I was on a slippery slope heading towards a negative cycle and inevitable hopelessness. I saw this contradiction as unfair for patients—that the type of disease patients experienced, determined the degree of respect and hope afforded to them.

During the radiation treatment, I followed the recommendations regarding regular physical activity to make sure the radiation could do its work. I kept diligently to my regular walking and incidental exercise during the day. Although I felt noticeably tired by the end of the treatment, I reminded myself that it was a tool that would help me in overcoming the cancer.

At the same time, my weight loss was proceeding on track and I was so pleased with my progress, that on the last day of radiation therapy, even though the radiation still had to peak, I doubled my cardio by walking in the morning and the evening as part of my routine.

I had read that the more weight you lose, the harder it is to keep losing it. In order to safely lose as much as possible within the first six months and beyond—and avoiding plateaus—I increased the pace and intensity of my exercise and continually monitored the range of food and my meal portions. I now walked briskly around the hills in my community that in earlier weeks seemed impossible. Walking to my local post office each afternoon to collect the business mail became part of my routine. This was a more demanding walk for 45 minutes than my morning program.

It was a very hot and humid summer and sometimes I felt exhausted by the end of the day. A few days after completing the radiation therapy, I broke out in a very painful, unsightly and extensive rash. It lasted for six weeks and refused to budge even with the use of a barrage of ointments, lotions and medications.

While I kept up my walking program twice daily, sometimes it was very uncomfortable. At times during the steamy days and humid nights, it was unbearable and only relieved by a cool shower at any time of the day or night. Then Annette suggested that the aloe vera plant might give me some relief. I had completely forgotten this neglected plant in my garden. I began to feel some relief within a day of using the gel straight from the plant. The rash that had at sometimes become blistered, and kept me awake at night, now lost its anger and within a week it had disappeared. Over the following year, I quickly fixed a few brief recurrences with this magical plant.

It now takes a prominent place in my garden with a new pot and regular watering!

Chapter Nine

Project Quality Management: Meeting Milestones

From my engineering clients, I had learned the importance of the critical pathway that was important in achieving project outcomes safely, cost-effectively and within time frames. They periodically used milestones to assess the progress of their project. Being mindful that there was a risk for a person to suffer another stroke or seizures within subsequent years, I was relieved when the 12-month milestone passed with no sign of these complications.

But unlike my engineering clients, I couldn't determine when my project would be completed—their bridge, building or road would finally be commissioned and handed over to the client— while my outcomes were indefinable. *How will I know that I'm on the right path to remain healthy for life?* To deal with this dilemma, I set milestones to assess my successes, and identify any problems that were obvious or could be predicted in the next phase of the project. This highlighted new opportunities, skills and behaviours that could be learned to keep me safe and healthy in a sustainable way, while continually tweaking and refining my new routines.

My lifestyle change was happening in reality—not just in my aspirations. I had new and unexpected interests, challenges and confidence, in my quest to emerge from the fog of my old life to a new life of positive possibilities. I had fewer down days as I felt more in control of my life again. I began to see new networks and links in my daily activities, their interdependence, and how changing a lifestyle was about building and sustaining connections, safely and cost-effectively, so they became automatic routines.

Losing a substantial amount of weight in itself raised other issues. I was frequently complimented on how I had lost weight, though to me my body image was still negative. I didn't yet fully trust myself to maintain all of these changes in the long term, so I ventured out to buy some clothes at local Op Shops to keep me reasonably dressed while I continued with weight loss. Finding some treasures and beautiful fabrics that had long since disappeared from our regular shops was good fun, even if they only lasted for a few weeks before I had to move to a lower dress size. I had told myself that I could simply keep the clothes that I enjoyed wearing as an OG, after having them altered by a local dressmaker. I still didn't value myself sufficiently to reward myself with new clothes that would suit my new body shape.

And it was changing. I had developed poor posture from slouching shoulders: constricted abdominal muscles had dragged them down as a result of sitting at a computer for years. I found that if I concentrated, I could stand straighter with shoulders back, breathe better, and feel more confident. I knew that walking straighter was also important in helping me to avoid osteoporosis, a potential side effect of the hormone therapy prescribed for the next five years by André, Medical Oncologist. There was good reason to make this change. So my walk also became my posture practice, working towards achieving a 'ballerina back.'

Within five months, my data sheets showed that I had moved from an OG, to a Fat Girl (FG).

Project Milestone: 5 Months

Physical Checks

Weight loss to date:	29 kilos
Weight loss expenditure:	Pedometer ($20), HFG Subscription ($49), Backpack ($65) = **Total $134**
BMI:	28.5
Waist:	93 cm
Eating:	Established wholefood pantry, no supplements or fad diets
Water intake:	Two litres each day
Daily Steps (walking):	Minimal 11 000 per day with up to 20 000 on Sundays
Exercise:	Regular walking each day with backpack weights (up to 8kg)
	WBAs throughout the day
	Up to five, 25-second segments of jogging during weekday walking
	Regular program changes
Sleep Pattern:	No short naps during the day
	Sleeping up to 5-6 hours uninterrupted most nights

Disease Recovery

Hypertension/Stroke:	Blood pressure mostly in normal limits
	Improved language fluency, reading, writing and comprehension
	Improved analytical skills
Auditory Processing:	Improving slowly

| Diabetes: | Reversed and blood sugar consistently within normal limits |
| Cancer: | Surgery successful. Radiation therapy to begin shortly |

Documentation

| Data Sheets: | Health data documented and updated daily |

Bonuses

Well-Being:	Feeling good! Calmer about life and its challenges
Physical:	No leg cramps or restless legs Good digestive health, no indigestion
Food Costs:	Consistently low
Dress Size:	16-18
Vegetable garden:	Good variety of successes for a beginner Enough spinach for Popeye

I found many different health measures all with varying attributes and flaws. I had little knowledge of how much weight I needed to lose, so using various measures highlighted a healthy trend. I could also see that weight loss, in isolation, could be misleading. I assessed my project at different milestones, drawing together these measures to identify progress.

Adele kept me focused on other behaviours that were vital to my well-being. She frequently reminded me to do lots of things more slowly, including speaking, to allow my brain to work better without becoming stressed. In endeavouring to apply her guidance across other areas of my changing lifestyle, I re-labelled my new way of eating learned during diabetes reversal, from a drill exercise to relaxation, slowing my breathing and improving my thinking processes. At first it had taken considerable self-control not to eat quickly—a habit I had learned from early years in the workforce. However, while developing greater insight into my own behaviour, I became aware of how I had used food to (often unsuccessfully) deal with stress. As I had now developed slow eating as my regular behaviour, I didn't have to count the chews, and was aware when I had eaten enough. I had become satisfied on smaller portions, learned to enjoy food better and looked on mealtimes and even snack times, as time for a break and relaxation.

Sometimes my weekly conversations with Adele centred on the way I could do things better to reduce my workload. The nature of my work still meant up to 12-hour workdays as I had done pre-stroke. The nature and intensity of my work hadn't changed. But the difference was that I was interspersing my work with frequent WBAs that forced me to take a break. I made the workday cut-off point around 10.00pm to develop a regular bedtime.

Our conversations also involved discussing my successes and challenges. They were true assessments of my progress in recovering my language; they involved discussions about the issues that were directly relevant to my life. It was an environment in which I could converse openly and comfortably. Between visits, I was always motivated by her optimism about my strategies in continuing to improve my procedures and routines, maximising the technology and looking for better outcomes from all the things that made up my day—whether personal or professional.

When Adele left after several months to pursue other interests, I declined her offer to find a replacement from the health system. Based on my experience, I was sceptical that her lateral-thinking and capacity to nurture my self-belief would be continued by conventional services. I felt confident that I could build on what she had taught me, by continuing to focus my attention on many issues of mind and body.

I felt privileged that I had benefitted from her ability to accurately assess my individual needs when I couldn't express them for myself. She supported me in rebuilding my independence and regaining control over my life—in my world—where I was most comfortable, and where overseas research showed there is a higher potential for success in stroke recovery. I knew I had been one of the lucky ones who had benefitted from the support of her skills, integrity and wisdom.

*

My auditory processing was slowly but steadily improving at home, at choir rehearsals and while out-and-about, and I became less anxious about it at gigs. I had overcome the fear of spontaneously interacting with other people, due to fear of missing their conversation. But I wanted to speed up the process of full recovery. So I deliberately exposed myself to other noisy environments or where there were lots of spontaneous and conflicting sounds to retrain my brain.

I had always enjoyed going to the movies, but in recent years there had been no time to enjoy this pastime. Now I treasured the time with friends on several occasions when we had dinner then visited a little local cinema. Initially, I found that the reverberation of the sound through the speakers made it almost impossible for me to understand the dialogue, even though I could clearly see the actors' faces.

Although it was frustrating in trying to concentrate and often struggling to follow the story, I was determined to use this as a tool in my recovery. I focused on the faces, actions and scenes to work out what was happening. But I often missed the subtle threads of the story, especially if the actor wasn't facing the camera.

When the little cinema changed to a digital system a few months later, I could understand the dialogue much better. What a pleasurable way to recover!

Beth, a choir member, invited me to a performance of *Grease* in a local theatre. This was my first test of interpreting sound in a live performance in a large space. I heard only one word clearly throughout the entire two-hour show, "Saaaandy!" I knew this was going to take longer than I thought!

I also accepted an invitation by Val and Nance and other members from choir to attend a monthly concert at a local club. We had dinner at the bistro, which put me in the midst of a large and very busy eating area, with multiple levels and types of voices and sounds. I forced myself to listen for familiar voices at the table above the noise, and concentrated on the visual cues. We sat in the middle of the auditorium for the concert. It was deafening: the loudness of the band, the reverberation of the sound system, the clinking of glasses, and general hubbub and noise of the large audience in a relatively small auditorium with low ceilings. I felt like I was next to a jet engine.

During the whole of the first concert I could understand only a few words—spoken or sung. I couldn't interpret what the singer was announcing because I couldn't clearly see his face because of the microphone, the distance from the stage and surrounding sound. As I couldn't understand the name of songs that he announced I tried to work out the name from my knowledge of the music as he sang. This was almost impossible with my brain struggling to keep up with the sound, except for the occasional phrase at the end of songs where he sang the words slowly.

The difficulty of remembering full names of people had plagued me from the earliest moments of the stroke—and it was similar with putting names to music that I knew. I couldn't converse with Val or Nance to comment on the concert, ask the name of the song or engage in other chatter during the performance, because I couldn't understand their reply above the noise.

When I looked back over six months of these concerts, I realised that I came a long way in improving my auditory processing disorder in a loud and reverberating environment. By then, I could mostly recognise the melodies shortly after the song started and understand much more of the singer's words, even if I frequently couldn't understand what was being said over the microphone. While this was sometimes a function of the singer's diction, I recognised that my brain was slowly becoming more attuned to sound differentiation in another noisy environment.

As I often drove Nance and Val to attend our choir gigs, their chatter in the car became good practice for me to hear and interpret their conversation, over the noise of the car and traffic. They laughed when I referred to them as my 'car therapists'.

*

I continued to integrate my recovery while walking at the lake and other locations. I noticed many people riding their bikes on the pathways, and I often wondered if I could ride a bike for additional exercise. I saw this as an opportunity to explore other parts of my newly discovered world, further afield than by walking. I hadn't ridden since childhood but I remembered it as very enjoyable, and easy, on a borrowed blue and yellow bike. I spoke to Craig from choir, and an avid cyclist, about the kind of bike I should buy. He offered to lend me an unused bike at home that could start me off with this new venture.

I was very excited when Craig and his wife Wendy arrived with the bike—it was royal purple with a white and green trim. How beautiful! I imagined riding around the lake, or on a recently opened, leafy, cycling track that had previously been a tramway near home, or even a cycling trip. He made sure it was the correct height and I resolved to practise riding the following day. (I tactfully refused his offer to ride with me at that moment, in case I fell off—and look like it was too hard for me).

The next day, wearing my new pink helmet, I set out determinedly for my first bike ride in more than 50 years. It was easy leaving home (it's true, you never lose the skill!) and I whizzed downhill to the first corner. I felt reasonably confident, though not expert, and set out for a ride of several kilometres to the next suburb, planning to hug the footpaths and stay off the road.

By the time I crossed the main road onto the pathway and cycled about half a kilometre on uneven concrete paths, I began to feel the strain. I walked the bike home. As enjoyable as it was being on a bike again, it was a long walk with legs that would hardly move and pushing the bike the final 200 metres up the steep hill to my home. I hadn't considered the years that had passed from when I rode the blue and yellow bike. Walking was sounding better than ever!

It was a few days before I had the stamina to try again. I read about the value of cycling as cardio exercise and that it would burn more calories than walking. This had the potential to extend the value of my exercise time by replacing some of my early morning walking with cycling. I resolved to ride at weekends initially, where I could take my time to learn how to handle the bike (and the gears), build my endurance and stamina in cycling—and enjoy the ride.

The next weekend I lifted the bike carefully into my car and drove it to the large car park and pathway at the lake. I rode around the car park and its garden areas for almost two hours, practising negotiating many obstacles to gain confidence. I was very pleased that I didn't fall off! Although I had no idea how to operate gears, *(do I really need them?)* I learned how to manoeuvre in and out of gateways, between barricades, around corners, across gutters, and on narrow paths—with legs that I could no longer feel. I left the bike in my car for the next weekend.

The following Saturday afternoon, I rode for a few kilometres on the shared path at the lake, carefully staying upright and avoiding the children, prams, dogs, people in deep conversation, and walkers with iPods who couldn't hear my bell. I also used some teachable moments while riding, to practise my language. I rang my bell as I rode closer to the walkers, while saying, "Bike passing on the right", in a firm voice. I stumbled a few times and laughed when I heard myself say, "Right bike" or "Pass right". Craig had mentioned to me that this was good practice even with ringing the bell. So I rehearsed as I rode until I did it correctly, every time. Then I extended my conversation with the walkers when they said, "Thank you" as I passed. I rehearsed a cheery response as I rode away, "It's OK. I'm a courteous cyclist". A few times it sounded like, "It's OK. I'm a 'cycleous' cyclist". Smiling to myself, I quickly fixed the error while I rode, practising my breathing and rhythm in my voice, so it sounded confident.

As I gathered pace, suddenly I discovered an unexpected problem. The improvement in differentiating sounds when walking, was useless when riding a bike. As I developed speed, the wind rushing past my ears combined with the noise of life on the lake, car engines on a busy nearby road and the incidental sounds of people in a popular recreation area, made it impossible for me to differentiate individual sounds unless I rode very slowly. I wanted to ride fast!

I began cycling again more often around my local community, so I could concentrate on training my brain to recognise the sound of cars behind me and become accustomed to environmental sound over the rushing wind. Fortunately, with little traffic in my local area I could practise with less risk. I integrated three bike rides each week into my exercise program by replacing morning or afternoon walks, while concentrating on differentiating sounds. This also provided more variation in my exercise program, in addition to a longer ride at weekends.

Nine months after the stroke, the choir was celebrating its 10th birthday. This was to be a large celebration attended by people from many other choirs. I was to be the accompanist for the evening.

Over the next few weeks, Annette and Lorraine built the anticipation of choir members with snippets of information about preparations for this important event. They planned a program full of meeting new people, sharing each other's company and lots of singing. But my anxiety grew. With between 200-300 guests singing with their voices clashing with the sound of the amplified piano, I knew that my brain—and my playing—would falter among the sound. *How can I play successfully at this event?* I had no answers and could only hope that I would survive the stress on the night.

And there was a further problem. *What will I wear?* Up until this point, clothes from Op Shops had enabled me to maintain a reasonable appearance as I rapidly lost weight. I hadn't bought any clothes suitable for a formal function.

Two weeks before the event I went shopping. I tried a little shop near the lake where I had often admired the clothes in the window as an OG. But now my reality was as a FG and I was almost an HG. The sales assistant was welcoming and helpful as I tried on several outfits. But the more I tried, the more the clothing looked wrong. I couldn't relate to the figure in the mirror. I realised that in all the years of denying myself the pleasure of beautiful clothes and keeping to simple styles, I had no idea what I liked or what suited my body shape, or what would make me feel good about myself. Having been used to wearing mass-produced shapeless clothing to cover my body shape, and with a brain that was still re-learning how to make decisions, I was lost.

I left the shop having made no purchase. I sat in the car, and cried. I cried with frustration at failing such a trivial task, at the HPs for wounding my self-confidence, the stroke for leaving me unable to think creatively, and the world for anything! *Am I frustrated because my injured brain can't think through and rationalise the experience? Am I still far from Bloom's creativity? Am I just out of practice?* I felt decidedly dejected, worthless, old, weak—and that it was all too hard. For a while I sat there and wallowed in valueless self-pity. But it didn't help.

It was still early in the day so I forced myself out of the quickly encroaching sadness—a looming down day—by thinking about my achievements. I thought about where I had struggled, and talked myself out of the fear of enjoying the upcoming event. Instead of driving home, I drove to a large shopping centre and vowed not to leave until I had found something that I could say, "That's it!"

When I arrived, I walked briskly around the Centre several times to do a reconnaissance, until I had triggered the endorphins, and proceeded in a positive frame of mind. My criteria were straightforward: simple, unfussy, suited to my age and goes with black pants. Three and a half hours later, with tired feet and a head full of different possibilities—laughable, ridiculous, beautiful and those with potential—I was back in my car with my treasures. I was feeling good! I had met some very knowledgeable, friendly and patient sales assistants who knew how to dress different body shapes for a formal occasion. I struggled with styles that were unfamiliar and that I would never have previously contemplated wearing. I learned a lot from their experience!

It briefly occurred to me that I hadn't spent any time coming to terms with a changing body image. But for that day, I had solved an immediate problem, and put the seed of this unfamiliar concept to the back of my mind.

Now for the next problem, how to cope with the sound on the night of the celebration? It was very important for my self-esteem and well-being to succeed at this event, in front of a large number of people who didn't know me, or my recent history. *Will they be disappointed in me if I don't play to the standard that I should?*

Four days before the event, becoming increasingly worried about what to do, I visited a shop selling musical equipment and asked for anything to help me. But all they could offer were large earphones. I couldn't see them being much help. I despaired that I might fail my own expectations.

But failure was not a concept that had ever been comfortable for me. On the spur of the moment on the way home, I called into a local Dick Smith Electronics store and by chance, spoke to Craig, a sales assistant, who was also a musician. I explained the problem and asked if there was anything that could solve the difficulty. *Is this co-incidence, or the universe working, that Adele had talked about?* He instantly empathised with my concern. He suggested wearing some tiny, noise-cancelling ear buds (reducing external sound by 87%)

used by people travelling in jets. He confidently assured me that they would work. At home I set up the piano, television and amp at high volume, put in the ear buds and began to play. He was right! For the first time since the stroke I could hear the music clearly and perfectly with hardly any background noise. I was so excited! The next day I went back to the shop and thanked him for his ingenuity and simple solution. He took the compliment modestly, but with a smile.

While wearing the ear buds at the celebration, only Annette knew that I could barely hear the singers. I could hear the piano and see her conducting, so I performed confidently throughout the night. I rejoiced at the success of such a tiny piece of technology. I was very grateful many times that night for Craig's lateral thinking.

Barb came along to the event and interpreted for me throughout the night when people spoke to me. Through many situations together during the preceding months, she had become adept in relaying other people's communication around me, when my brain became lost. At the celebration, she took on the role of being my 'ears'. To be part of the vibrant atmosphere was exhilarating. I had a fleeting recollection of less than 12 months earlier wondering if I could ever leave my home. On the way home, we laughed at our success in having an enjoyable night out by using a few simple tools to get around a debilitating and frustrating disorder. In a great leap forward for my sense of well-being, I had freely and happily participated in life alongside good friends. It was a celebration, and a milestone, from many different perspectives!

Project Milestone: 10 Months

Physical Checks

Weight loss to date:	45 kilos
Weight loss expenditure:	Joggers ($165), Stepper $45 (for wet weather) = **Total: $210**
BMI:	22.6: Healthy Girl (HG)—a 'Hot Girl' said Lyn, choir member.
Waist:	76cm
Eating:	Well-established wholefood pantry
Water intake:	Minimum 2.5 litres each day
Daily Steps:	Minimum 11 000 per day with up to 20 000 on Sundays
Exercise:	Walking minimum 2 hours each day, with 3-4 hours on Sundays WBAs throughout the day to keep active Up to five 30-second segments of jogging/shuffle in an hour. Cycling 2-3 times per week and weekends
Breathing Patterns:	Good breath control while speaking
Sleep Pattern:	Up to 7 hours uninterrupted sleep each night

Recovery from Illness

Hypertension/Stroke:	Good language articulation, rhythm and intonation Improved higher level thinking on Bloom's Taxonomy Only occasional stumbles and rare black holes Blood pressure maintained in normal limits
Auditory Processing:	Manageable and much improved

Diabetes:	Blood sugar consistently within normal limits
Cancer:	Radiation therapy completed
	Hormone therapy commenced

Documentation

| Data Sheets: | Health data documented daily |
| | Regular program changes and updates as required |

Bonuses:

Well-Being:	Positive outlook
	Confidently participating in life
Physical:	Good digestive health
	No leg cramps
	No restless legs at night prior to sleeping
	No indigestion
	No fasciitis
	No arthritic pain in wrist and finger joints (or any other joints)
	No buffalo hump between shoulders
	No low back discomfort
Food Costs:	Consistently low
Vegetable and herb garden:	Productive and easy to manage
Dress size:	Small, 8-10
Clothing Style:	Anything I like
Waist:	Found for the first time since my early 20s
Ballerina Back:	Getting easier to hold in place without thinking
Shoulder Bag:	Stays in place for the first time in 40 years
Joggers:	Worn out for the first time in my life

Chapter Ten

Project Review: Reality Check

Although I hadn't set a specific target for my weight loss, I had now lost almost half of my body weight. I was a Healthy Girl (HG). *Is this enough weight loss? It fits with the BMI and blood glucose maintained well within the ideal levels.* I had also educated myself to understand each line on my pathology results—they were beautiful numbers. It was surreal to see the data on my Health Data Sheet changing and improving through my meticulous daily entries. This was the reality that I had longed for over many years. I could feel my shoulder bones and ribs for the first time in at least 40 years. I realised that I had lost fat from everywhere—not only from where it was obvious—but even from my head, face, ears, hands and feet. Everything physical about me was smaller, trimmer and healthier. The evidence was there. Ken was very pleased and gave me a "gold star".

As I was clearly in a new healthy lifestyle, I considered a tangible reward was in order. During my intensive exercise program I had worn old shorts and tees for sustained, brisk walking in the humidity and heat of summer. I had sweated profusely. I had wondered if my clothes (mostly cotton) had exacerbated the painful rash that had occurred shortly after the radiation treatment. Somewhere, I had read about the value of wicking fabric. It occurred to me that I could keep up the exercise in any weather if my clothing didn't feel uncomfortable (or perhaps it was an excuse to buy some new clothes!)

I ventured to Lorna Jane Activewear to buy some exercise clothes made from wicking fabric. Walking in as an HG was a very different experience to admiring the clothing through the window. I immediately felt like an old woman among the perky young customers. I was clearly the oldest person in the shop by several decades. I walked around calmly and slowly, looking nonchalantly at the garments and listening to the way the young sales assistants spoke to their customers. They sounded friendly and helpful. *But can I relate to them? Will they think I'm crazy asking for sportswear at my age?* Taking a deep breath, I approached Tanya who was walking out of the changing room area accompanying a clearly happy customer. I explained to her briefly why I was there: "I'm looking for wicking fabric in quality sportswear, to prevent a recurrence of what may have been a nasty heat rash." If these requirements were new to her from older women customers, she didn't look fazed about finding the clothes I needed.

As I waited in the change room for her to return with some clothes to try, I thought that even though I had lost 45kg, how stereotypical I looked as an older woman. *I don't want to look like an old girl squeezed into tight sportswear meant for young people—with bulges everywhere trying to find a way out.* This confronting body image was prominent in my mind.

I reminded myself that I hadn't considered the issue of body image to any significant degree when finding clothes for the choir celebrations several weeks earlier. Perhaps my brain was too caught up with self-pity to think rationally. Then, I had used my 'safe' criteria for selecting clothes that I had used for as long as I could remember—just smaller.

Now, standing in front of a full-length mirror, for the first time in many years, visualising trying on a style of clothing that was designed for much younger women, reinforced the negative body perception that I had lived with for many years. I had long ago disposed of a full-length mirror at home in a Council pickup. That way I didn't have to face how unhealthy I looked while carrying so much weight. And now I was also aging. I couldn't see the difference that had been made by my weight loss. It was confronting!

But within minutes of trying on some items, I felt a boost to my self-esteem when I realised the difference. Tanya smiled, knowing her products well. All of a sudden I had shape. *I can remember having a figure like this at 18 in a school formal photograph!* With some careful and strategic dressing suited to my new shape, the leftovers disappeared, and I saw my new reality—a fit and healthy woman with an ideal weight. I felt good! The fabrics felt beautiful and increased my sense of energy, comfort and confidence.

On the way home, I laughed about the idea of wearing stylish sportswear at my age. During the next few days, the fabric fulfilled my expectations when I wore it during my hot afternoon walks. I arrived home less exhausted and feeling comfortable, rather than being soaked with perspiration. When I experienced a hot flush as a side effect of the hormone therapy, it was almost unnoticeable. I threw out my old OG cotton shorts and tees.

On another occasion at another branch of the store, I met Lisa who took the time to assist me in selecting other pieces for my new sportswear wardrobe. From those early days, I learned the value of wearing these beautiful fabrics and styles every day for my early morning exercise program and at other times during long days alone in my office editing and writing. Being dressed and ready made it easy to integrate my work with my active WBAs during the day.

A few weeks after my sportswear shopping trips, the issue of body image again reminded me that my brain was still grappling with this issue. I had called into a little boutique in a large shopping centre and found some clothes suitable for work. The sales assistant invited me to try them on in any one of the cubicles. As I walked past the first one, it was full. The second one was full. Then a woman emerged from what looked like the fourth cubicle, and quickly walked towards me. I stepped left and she followed; I stepped right and she followed. I then stepped forward to go quickly around her and—*crash*—ran into the full-length mirror. I turned to see the sales assistant looking puzzled and quickly slipped into the third cubicle with a quiet laugh. My excuse for not recognising myself? It was dim light and I was in a rush!

Perhaps the universe stepped in, because a few weeks later, Ben, an Exercise Physiologist client, called me to assist him with some career development. I hadn't seen him for a few years since his foray into the health and fitness industry. He was very supportive of all I had done to improve my health, and was very surprised at my changed physical appearance. He explained that weights would help me tone up the weak and sagging muscles and provide balance with the intensive cardio exercise that I had used to lose so much weight.

Within a few days, and with education on how to use weights safely, I had a program that I could do at home. Now I had some dumb bells, a stability ball and a gym mat. At first, the weights felt very heavy—just like lifting 3-litre milk bottles! *How can I do this repeatedly for a series of exercises?* I took it slowly. I couldn't manage the full list of sets and reps that Ben had set up for me initially, so I gradually built up my stamina through as many as I could manage, then added one more. He assured me that a 'slow muscle wakeup' was the strategy. He also explained the value of exercise after, rather than before breakfast, to maximise the availability of energy during the exercise. I also realised that this was preferable to using breakfast as a reward for exercise, because of the potential to eat more if I was very hungry after returning home.

I began to really enjoy the weights program. By making it a priority I re-organised my work days so that I spent up to 45 minutes 2-3 times each week on weights. I felt the energised fatigue after each session. Over several months I could see the benefits in my improved physical strength.

Over time, Ben renewed my program to keep me interested with heavier weights, a more flexible program and more challenging exercises. Doing weights became another non-negotiable activity in my project. The feeling of self-confidence, vitality and health from doing functional exercise every day, was too precious to lose by non-compliance and falling back into old habits. I was starting to see some physical changes in toned arms, legs and body that I had never imagined I could possess. For the first time in my life, I was heading towards abs!

*

It was hard to believe that almost 12 months had passed since the stroke. I wanted to mark this anniversary with something positive, and symbolically leave behind the barriers that had sometimes plagued me during my recovery. *Will I come to a grinding halt as suggested by some HPs—and 'plateau'?* I dismissed this negativism by HPs as having no place in my plan. I knew that motivating myself to keep going by constantly stimulating my brain was the best weapon I had to ensure that it didn't happen. I had too much to live for and so many things to do in my new life.

I decided that I could challenge myself by learning a classical piece of music, and perform it for the choirs. As a young pianist, my showpiece had been Singding's 'Rustle of Spring'. I had played it at many public performances, and had never tired of learning more about how it created such emotion and beautiful mind pictures. I had loved the piece from the first time Ellie, my inspiring music teacher, had played it for me. I remembered asking her to play it for me several times so I could absorb the beauty of the music. *Can I relearn it and perform it in a few weeks, with my still fragile brain?* I found several videos on YouTube and watched them to find the one that most resembled the way I had played it. And after searching for almost two hours in my music library, I found my original sheet music.

I studied the score with great fondness, and broke it down into several sections, then broke those sections into smaller phrases. Although my brain had improved significantly in linking things together, my first tentative steps were very poor in playing the music so that it flowed. After more than 40 years, although I had forgotten the parts that were particularly difficult, on my music were still the pencil-written reminders from Ellie of what to do in tricky segments.

I felt daunted by the task: to re-learn eight pages of music comprising many intricacies and sections requiring good technique. I imagined Adele saying, "It's patience, Alana".

I started very slowly and deliberately bar-by-bar, line-by-line, and section-by-section. I frequently practised for 5-10 minutes as weekday WBAs. I set small tasks knowing that I could concentrate better for shorter periods. At weekends I spent longer practice periods in refining and polishing each section.

Sometimes, I wondered why I would put myself through this challenge and the accompanying stress. But on the other hand, I wanted to prove to myself—and anyone who doubted my motivation and self-discipline—that I could accomplish a complex task regardless of gloomy predictions.

Ten days ahead of the anniversary I had practised to a reasonable level of competence. Now I needed an audience for a dress rehearsal before the real performance. So I organised a recital at home with a posh morning tea for a small group of friends that had supported me through all the ups and downs in the past year. Having learned the pressure of performance so many years ago, I saw this as the best test of whether my brain had recovered some of the more complex skills: planning, analysing, problem-solving, and using my creativity and concentration in a high-pressure situation.

While my performance at our little recital wasn't without flaws, overall I was very pleased with the outcome. We celebrated our combined effort during my project with a beautiful morning tea. It had taken me two days to prepare scrumptious goodies, from making my own baked ricotta cheese, to delicate sandwiches fit for royalty, and creative canapés. The recital was an opportunity for me to thank them for their faith in me, and highlight my indebtedness to all of them for their unconditional support.

The following week, I performed Rustle of Spring for both choirs in a very emotional atmosphere. As I played, I could feel the adrenaline spurring my confidence to conquer this challenge. My wonderful audiences responded with profound warmth. It highlighted the value of friendship and caring for each other that had always been the hallmark of the choirs. There were no words that I could say to thank them enough at those performances for their generosity of spirit, prayers, and love shown to me in the past year. But they could see that the effort they had put into supporting me had a real and tangible outcome. I also baked several varieties of ANZAC cookies for supper, made quickly and efficiently with hardly a glance at the recipe.

Several months later, the choir was invited to provide the entertainment for two hours at a large recreational club on a Sunday afternoon. Three weeks ahead of the day, Annette casually asked me if I could do a piano piece as one of the items on the program. *Three weeks!* After the euphoria of my Rustle of Spring performance I had settled into a feeling of achievement. *Can I learn something else in a short time frame?* I went to my music collection and looked for a piece that might entertain club members. After a lengthy search I came across 'Cumana', a piece that I had never played. I set myself a new challenge: learn a totally new piece to performance standard, and play it without the music. *I will prove to myself that my earlier performance had been more than luck.*

So I began to break down the music, in my tried and tested strategy. I watched it on YouTube, studied the scope of the music, worked on it slowly, built it bar-by-bar, phrase-by-phrase, section-by-section then joined up the sections. *Treat it like a conversation among a group!* Ellie had used this old-fashioned way of teaching me a new piece and giving it character. I spent many hours during my WBAs as well as before and after work hours, ploughing through the music and at times wondering if I had selected the right piece.

A week before the concert it was slowly coming together, except for the tricky middle section that needed much more work. I had to make a decision. I streamlined the middle section so it was more playable. I started polishing the piece, with enough time to learn to play without music.

During the concert program as the choir sang, I edged closer to my performance time. It was a busy club with a large audience. *Can I do this? Will I make a fool of myself? What if I forget the music?* The butterflies were alive and fluttering at a furious pace. I knew I had to have them flying in formation in order to get through this challenge.

As Annette announced my performance I took a few deep breaths and moved into the zone. I had practised visualising playing the piece many times during the previous days. Now was the real test. I concentrated as hard as I could to focus on the conversation of the music, and began to play with gusto. I looked at the piano intently, following the 'speakers' through the music, and creating the vibrant Latin rhythm. I was oblivious of the club and the audience, and became lost in the energy of the music, finishing with a flourish Liberace-style! I was ecstatic that I had played completely without music, kept my brain focused without losing track from start to finish, and enjoyed the experience! It was the familiar energised fatigue that I had experienced so many times from my exercise. I soaked up the euphoria again and relished my success. I knew I had jumped another milestone in my recovery.

Project Milestone: 24 Months

Physical Checks

Weight loss to date:	45 kg
Weight loss expenditure	Weights ($110), mat ($8), stability ball
BMI:	($50) = **Total $168**
	22.4 (HG)
Waist:	78cm
Eating:	Thoroughly enjoying and managing a well-functioning gourmet wholefood pantry.
Water intake:	Minimum 2 litres per day.
Exercise:	Regular walking and/or cycling daily for around 2 hours.
Weights	2-3 times each week.
WBAs:	Scattered systematically throughout each day.
Sleep:	Significantly improved, uninterrupted 7-8 hours per night.

Recovery from Illness

Stroke:	Language and associated skills fully recovered.
Auditory Processing:	Vastly improved in most settings.
Cancer:	All positive results.
Diabetes:	Reversed and blood sugar maintained within normal limits.
Documentation:	Health data maintained daily.
Bonuses	Confidently participating in life.
	A feeling of health, strength and vitality.
	Met physical measurements to be a US Marine (lol).

Chapter Eleven

Project Maintenance: Moving to the Next Level

With my project having achieved far more than I had dared possible, I knew it was essential to set systems in place for long-term maintenance. It was time to revisit the risks that could ultimately lead to project failure.

Risk: **Losing motivation for exercise**
Solution: **Continuously changing and improving my exercise program and the range of activities**

In order to sustain the change in lifestyle behaviours, especially with exercise, I knew that my motivation had to be closely linked to recognisable benefits. The lifelong view for me was to make sure that I had sufficient and safe variation in exercise during older age. The challenge was to avoid returning to old and destructive habits, stress and obesity through inactivity.

At the beginning of the project, I used walking as the only structured exercise for weight loss. It achieved this purpose. But as my exercise program extended to include cycling, I knew that to use the convenience of an exercise bike at home meant that it was too easy to get off the bike, and do something else less active. But if I was walking or cycling outdoors, I had to keep moving in order to get home. And I knew I needed variety to keep me interested and challenged.

I appreciated that this was not the way everyone thought of exercise, particularly if they preferred the role models around them in the gym to keep motivated. For me, I knew there was a greater probability that I would keep up the exercise if done on my own, in a more natural way. There was a lot of research that describes why people start at a gym and often drop away after initial enthusiasm. But what role models would I find among the majority of people of my age?

There was little that I could find in my local area for older people who wanted to work at a more active level rather than the expectation of increasing 'slowness'. Although I had become accustomed to daily brisk walking, regular cycling, and a few minutes of tai chi into my early morning wakeup stretching exercise, I needed something more stimulating. I was unwilling to give up my renewed energy at that point and settle back to what was seen as 'safe exercise' often associated with aging.

Even Ken, when I showed him my Health Data Sheet, cautioned, "Sarcopenia (a gradual loss of muscle integrity) is common and a natural result of aging". This could limit my activity. *Can I delay sarcopenia?* I found many articles suggesting the possibility. While I appreciated Ken's guidance, I promptly took a pathway to see whether it was possible for me.

By this time, I easily implemented my regular walks each day, cycling, weights program and WBAs, as priorities and routines. *Is this enough to sustain and motivate me for the next twenty years or so? Is there enough variety? Will aging allow me to continue in these pursuits?* I wanted, and found, more.

I looked at what I was doing with walking and wondered how I could vary or intensify this part of my program, but still work within my scheduled time for exercise. *Can I run?* Aside from a few spasmodic seconds of a rather limited form of jogging during my walks, I hadn't extended this to more functional exercise. One Saturday morning I went to a sporting oval near my home to give it a try. On the grassy surface and with no preparation or knowledge of what I was doing, I began to run—not too fast and not too hard—around the perimeter. To my surprise, I made it once around the oval quite comfortably. I decided to do a running circuit of the oval during my next morning walk.

The following day, I went almost twice around the oval at the beginning of the walk. I came home feeling like I had moved to another level of exercise with no ill effects. But by that afternoon I could feel pain in my right knee. *Maybe I'm too old to run.* Ben suggested that I had done too much intensive exercise too quickly and without knowing about technique. It was almost six weeks before my knee felt completely pain-free. During that time I walked every day, but didn't attempt to run.

Although it was a brief venture, I had nevertheless experienced the good feeling that comes from running. Once the pain had subsided, I thought about the possibility of varying my experience with this much more demanding activity, but in a more measured way. *Is it really possible for me to run at my age?* I started reading about how to run safely and found that there were numerous credible articles that highlighted the benefits of running for older people. Some even suggested it could slow down the aging process. A check of the Masters' Games program showed that people much older than me were runners. Not all of them had been running for years.

Over the next few weeks, I followed some well-structured running programs on YouTube. I slowly began to build my technique until I was running for almost half of my early morning walking time. I didn't run fast, but I really began to enjoy relaxed running.

I no longer had to lose any weight, but there was room to build my stamina and endurance so I could continue to vary my exercise in different ways. My strategy had always been to maximise the benefit from the time I allocated to exercise.

One Friday morning, I noticed a new sign on a telegraph pole shortly into my walking and running combo. It advertised 'parkrun', a 5km run at the lake on Saturday mornings. *Is the universe working again?* In all the months that I walked to lose weight I didn't calculate the distance that I walked each day. I knew it was more important to focus on the quality of the walk rather than the length. I was interested to know how it felt to run 5km. I registered that night. I turned up the following morning, at Lake Mac parkrun, to find a very large group of people ready for the run.

I ran as I had been practising, but found that I was comparatively slow, although I was by no means last. Surrounded by a large group of other runners of many different ages, shapes and sizes, I felt motivated to run faster than I had done at home. Within the first 400 metres I could feel tightness in my chest. It was uncomfortable but settled over the next kilometre as I focused on breathing rhythmically. I was exhausted at the end but had the feeling of energised fatigue. That day my recorded time was 55.22.

Hmm.... can I do better than that?

By the next weekend I had researched diaphragmatic breathing to prevent the tightness and maintain energy, and how to use correct arm movement to give me momentum and body placement while running. I practised in my driveway during WBAs. In a short run after dinner on two evenings, I implemented what I learned. The following weekend I dropped my parkrun time by more than eight minutes to a new Personal Best (PB).

I began running at parkrun each week, only interrupted by the occasional wet weather. I set my strategy to plan each section of the run, hugging the corners where I could, conserving my energy on the gentle rises in the path and using gravity to help me on the downward gradients. I used other runners as my pacers—some much younger OBs and FGs—or people around my age with good technique and a steady pace. I continued to search YouTube, then learned and improved my technique. I was fascinated by the science of running. After 20 parkruns, my PB was recorded at 30.16, 25 minutes below my first time. I was now often first in my age category. I looked forward excitedly to receiving my results each week on email. It was motivating to see the graph gradually showing improvement.

As I gained confidence, I frequently replaced walking with running during my daily cardio exercise. To keep my interest I mixed and matched my twice daily combination of walking, cycling or running with various routes, now taking on the steep hills around my home to build my stamina. I began frequently running to my local post office to collect the business mail. This meant following a route I couldn't imagine that I could walk as an OG. Now, as an HG, I could run comfortably more than 5km regularly, with demanding hills and different terrains.

During this period, I read an article suggesting that as we age, nature teaches us to look down to avoid hazards that may cause us to fall. But the article went further to suggest that unfortunately, this often leads to poor posture. Over time, it can become harder to retain mobility. The eyes take over the role of keeping us safe and our feet become less aware of recognising and responding naturally to the terrain. For many people, there is an inevitable transition to a walking stick and/or some other form of mobility aid.

In an aging population, this is evident in the huge growth of the mobility aids industry, accompanied by aggressive advertising. In reality it can be seen in any shopping centre with the number of older people with many forms of mobility vehicles and other aids. For me, I was also reminded of the potential for loss of bone density and osteoporosis from hormone medication, prescribed by André for five years following the cancer treatment.

I decided to conduct my own observation of this slow decline. I drove to the car park overlooking the ocean where there was a steep pathway frequented by many walkers. With a delicious picnic lunch from my pantry and a thermos of tea, I sat in the park and observed the behaviour of the walkers. It was a beautiful sunny Saturday afternoon and I was captivated by the freshness of the salty air, the seagulls that kept a watchful eye on my lunch, and the chatter of the walkers. I watched people of all ages for more than an hour and noted whether or not they were looking up or down on the pathway coming downhill between two points. I was amused to find that it seemed like the article had been correct. The only exception was that many young people moved quickly down the path looking downwards—texting!

Perhaps this little observation exercise, albeit completely unscientific, was an excuse to visit the beach for a relaxing afternoon. But as I sat there soaking up the sunlight, I wondered if I could delay this inevitable decline? *Can I continue to be healthier and fitter for longer than might be expected, to maintain muscle and bone integrity?* Armed with these questions and after reading more on calcium-rich foods, I found that I easily exceeded the amount of recommended calcium in my gourmet menu each day. I had kept up with a vigorous and varied exercise program that included substantial resistance training—ideal for maintaining strong bones, and achieved with no supplements. My bone density test at the beginning of hormone therapy showed normal results. (Almost three years later, I had lost only 1% in my bone density; far less than clinical research studies had shown over five years). Ken and André were pleased with the result and I knew my tools of exercise and nutrient-rich foods were doing their respective jobs.

To work a little harder at this, I began walking around without shoes at home, as often as possible, to make my brain connect with my feet by becoming aware of different surfaces. At first, I found it uncomfortable to walk outside without shoes, but I realised that with every step I was becoming more conscious of the ground and the strength in my legs. I persisted with walking over different surfaces, even when I occasionally stepped on a sharp stone, but it gradually became easier. I became more aware of how my brain and muscles worked together to improve my health and well-being. It became easier to keep my back straight and to be conscious of it when I walked, ran or when I sat at the computer or the piano.

A two-hour choir rehearsal was a good test of my stamina in practising my new physical techniques. As an OG over many years I had often experienced back pain from poor posture at the piano and a seat with no back. Now I found that I could comfortably sit with straighter posture for two hours and the back pain disappeared.

I began to concentrate on my running technique and by following a few useful tips, found that I could run further, breathe easier and really enjoy the run.

I taught myself a little slogan: 'See it. Plan it. Do it'. I learned to love the feeling of running around the streets—with shoes—doing interval training. Where there were some broken concrete paths and long grass in the cracks posed potential hazards, I stayed upright, never tripped and lightly sidestepped the obstacles.

Eight months after starting parkrun, I saw an advertisement for a Fun Run at the lake to be held the following day. *How does it feel to run 10.5k?* I couldn't visualise how far it was to run. *Could I make it?* By late that night, I had convinced myself that if I ran out of energy along the way, I could walk. I registered online. After a small but delicious high-carb / high-protein smoothie for an early breakfast, I turned up at 6.30am to organise my late entry.

There were many competitors already there and I felt excited at the challenge ahead. I walked around the area to soak in the noise, the 'busyness' of the organisers, excited participants, and the ambience of the lake on a beautiful August morning. As the day began to wake, the crowd quickly swelled both on and off the run route. There was excited chatter, and a high sense of enthusiasm among the runners and the crowd of onlookers. I kept myself limbered up with stretching exercises, and tried to look like a calm, seasoned athlete. I felt the anticipation as I joined the very large crowd at the starting point.

I knew I had to pace myself. At the signal, I set off at a leisurely speed getting my breathing and arms working correctly. The beautiful morning and the crisp air were very stimulating and it was easy to quickly fall into a rhythm. It was intoxicating with the feeling that I was on my own but sheltered by a crowd, not burdened by any expectations and exploring a whole new venture. I experienced the surreal feeling again that I had felt many times. *Is this really happening? Am I really running?*

I kept going. Sometimes I passed other runners who were now walking. Sometimes I used other runners as unwitting pacers to keep up. Just as I had found at parkrun, some younger runners could even run at pace while talking! I maintained rhythm in my running and breathing, focusing on the mechanics to avoid wondering how much further there was to run.

As I sprinted downhill and along the road towards the halfway point (I reminded myself that I had to run back up this hill to get to the finish line!), a quick drink on the go as I started the ascent, and I was on the way home. It seemed far longer than when coming down, as the road meandered its way around the long and sweeping curves on the edge of the lake. The salty air, sounds of the birds, excited dogs running the route pulling their owners along, and the breeze in my face, took me to another place. I stashed my glasses (slipping down with sweat) in my pocket, so I could savour the full spectrum of sensory stimulation—be in the moment—drawing on everything I could to keep up my stamina.

The road that was so familiar to me as a driver now seemed different as a runner. As the hill continued to climb and I tired, I used my strategy of hugging the corners, pushing myself to achieve the next 50 metres, or around the next curve, or past the next telegraph pole, or up to the next street corner—then kept going. Perhaps I allowed my mind to wander a little from the task as I reminded myself of how my newfound skills and ways of thinking were opening new experiences. I smiled to myself as I reached the top of the hill and appreciated that my life was now full of new and unimagined adventures.

Back to reality! With the long hill conquered, I settled into a comfortable pace to reach the finishing line. Someone yelled out from the sidelines, "Good on you No. 2205! Keep it up!" I waved in acknowledgement. What a hoot! I was spurred to keep going—perhaps it was another senior runner!

I was feeling decidedly less energetic by the time I came in sight of the finishing line. But I applied my parkrun strategy—focus on finishing the run without stopping or walking, and let the PB take care of itself. I finished the Fun Run in 1 hour and 26 minutes. I was very pleased with myself. I felt like an elite athlete!

I rewarded myself with a skinny cappuccino at the Gardenia Café at Lee Rowan's Gardenworld. I could feel the adrenaline and my muscles working for a long time afterwards, in a positive and energising way. I felt very healthy, and read the newspaper and relaxed for an hour or so with my coffee and a litre of cool water. I thought about the thrill of spontaneous achievement that had come from an unplanned activity.

Fit and healthy at a 10.5km Fun Run

After almost a year at parkrun, I looked around at where there was a more challenging venue. Frank mentioned Lakeview parkrun near his home, and cautioned that it was very testing. That was enough for me! The following Saturday I lined up with the group.

This venue was a complete contrast to my usual flat location at Lake Mac.

While waiting to start, I stood near a father instructing his two young daughters on altering their breathing and running pattern while running uphill. I tried his idea and found that it helped in maintaining strength and endurance on very steep hills. And I found them! Long winding tracks uphill wound their way through the bush and finally downhill into a beautiful rainforest area.

I was enthusiastic about my conquest of hills as my running had improved in my local community, and I enjoyed the variation that this new track brought to my weekly run. I relished the smells of the lake, the bush, the sounds of the rainforest that rushed at me as I sprinted along the track, and the motivating calls of the marshall at the halfway point urging us to keep going.

Later, I added the Bluegum Hills venue into my parkruns with an even more difficult track with no concrete paths, just gravel and grass in a bushland reserve. I became confident in running without my glasses, so that my feet and brain had to continually connect on the tricky and uneven terrain. What a great feeling of power forging through strong leg muscles, knee joints and feet sprinting down the hills at speed. It was almost as good as whizzing down the hills on my bike!

At Lakeview and Bluegum Hills my name was often printed at the top of the list of runners' results—not as the winner, but as the oldest!

Parkrun also brought with it new friends, sharing the love of running and encouraging each other—especially among senior runners. I was delighted when a young woman thanked me for being her unwitting pacer. She said she found it difficult to keep up with me. That was surreal!

Each week, I relished the adrenaline rush, building up to the final burst at the end and running through the funnel to the clapping and cheers of the volunteers. I welcomed the coolness of the wet towel and the even cooler jazz in the car, driving back to my weekly coffee treat and morning newspaper. The sense of euphoria became precious each weekend, relaxing in my quiet corner at the Gardenia Café.

My Sunday walk then evolved into my Sunday run/walk at a gentle pace, with no timing, no pressure, just enjoying the fresh, clear air and ambience of the lake for up to 10kms.

As I lost my dogs through illness and old age during the next 12 months, I used my Sunday walk as a means of obtaining a 'dog fix'—occasionally stopping to talk to some of the many dogs (and their owners) enjoying their Sunday morning walk.

Keeping my interest in exercise became easy, with such variety available, and free of charge. I found many different parkruns, walking and cycling tracks to keep me interested for years to come.

Risk:	**Aging**
Solution:	**Keep working with it and using creative ways to enjoy it, but don't give up.**

On the continuous road of educating myself about healthy lifestyle, I came across an article talking about balance. About two years into the project, I read in the *Healthy Food Guide* magazine that aging brought increased risk of falls and complications. When I tried the simple activities in the article to test my balance, especially those with my eyes closed, I didn't pass them as well as I expected. *Is this an outcome of the stroke? Is this the natural process of aging? Is it the result of decades of limited activity, obesity and less than desirable health?*

I then read further and discovered balance could be improved by various activities, mostly done in a gym and/or under the supervision of an HP. I looked for an alternative.

While driving to a choir gig I noticed a street sign, 'danceVibe: Learn to Dance' on the footpath near a local club. *Is this the universe working again?* This seemed like a perfectly enjoyable way to naturally improve balance. Having been a follower of dance in many forms for as long as I could remember, I had always imagined it to be good fun to dance socially. But aside from a few years learning ballet as a child, I hadn't been in a situation as an adult to explore dancing as a form of recreation or exercise. I didn't know what type of dance was done at danceVibe. *Perhaps it's the dancing people did in clubs during my earlier years as a professional musician. Too slow!* But I reminded myself that if I didn't like it, I could leave!

The following night I arrived with excited anticipation in the club's auditorium. The dance was advertised as modern jive. *Are these 'bobby-soxers' and throwing-the-girl-over-the-shoulder type of dance of the 40s and 50s?* The music was lively and there were some people already on the dance floor, clearly enjoying the music and their dancing. There were adults of all ages, levels of skills and experience. I was relieved to see that they had come a long way from the bobby-soxers. They were fascinating, lively, quirky and happy. *Can I learn to do that?*

Within a few minutes, Adrian, the Director, took to the stage with a partner to demonstrate the steps while everyone else gathered in the auditorium for the lesson. I followed the crowd, with women lining up in several columns around the room facing the men.

As soon as Adrian began to speak, I knew I was in trouble. It was a very large auditorium, with loud speakers to amplify his directions and the music. The sound was deafening. All I could do was watch and follow what I saw, rather than rely on his voice. The sound reverberated around my head and my brain had difficulty in coping with the sound. I was too far away from the stage to see his face clearly to understand his conversation. I could feel the anxiety accelerating. I had no idea what he was saying. *Will I look silly if I can't follow the directions?*

He proceeded to teach us the first of three steps. I watched carefully, falling back on my observational skills that had supported me from the first day of the stroke. *Concentrate to get rid of the noise. Focus on his movement. Each step has several components.* As the lesson was done in a progressive style, we quickly moved around the dance floor, meeting a new person every few seconds. Some experienced dancers and instructors scattered through the group realised that I was a first-timer, and welcomed me with a friendly chat along the way.

Concentrating as hard as I could helped me to practise each step in a sequence of three, which then brought us back to the beginning for a repeat. This was instantly very demanding. I smiled, looking as if I was confident in learning completely unfamiliar and sometimes complex steps. I responded in a courteous manner even though I couldn't hear what they said over the music. I apologised when I stepped on their feet, kept moving forward in the right direction after turning in a loop and remembered how to follow the directions for linking each step. This was multi-tasking at a whole new level. I loved it!

I had learned through past experiences that I could generally get around my auditory problems through some creative thinking. After taking a few deep breaths, I reminded myself that I didn't need to feel intimidated or lacking in this new situation. I rationalised and talked myself out of the potential anxiety by reminding myself that everyone was in the same situation: learning and practising new skills. *I've proven that I can do that!* I relied intently on watching Adrian and his partner and the people around me in order to learn. There was no mandate for me to be good at dancing. *Just enjoy it!* This entirely new activity had any benefits. It fulfilled the need for me to be active, challenge my brain to learn and remember new skills, interact with new people, and thoroughly enjoy myself as part of life. It was great therapy!

When a partner I had passed by in the progressive lesson asked me for a dance during free-dance time, I was eager to test myself in remembering the sequences, and tried my best to do the steps well.

Fortunately, he was a more experienced dancer. He gave me confidence by leading me expertly through the dance without stepping on his toes, while politely suggesting to me how to do the steps better. As I relaxed into the dance it became easier. I began to recognise the subtle hand and body movements that led into another step, as we repeated the three steps continuously through the music. I felt like I was in a dream. I whirled quickly, turned and changed direction till I was almost giddy—while retaining my balance. I laughed at my feeble attempts to link the steps with a brain that struggled to remember new linkages. When the free-dance music finished and we resumed the dance lesson with some polishing of the three steps, I had a sense of achievement in my new skills. I stayed for two hours on that first night.

I arrived home with a sense of elation, far too excited to sleep. Dancing was all the fun that I had imagined. While making a cup of tea, I tried to remember the three intricate steps. I found that my brain had almost forgotten them, but the fantastic feeling remained. I decided to make the weekly dance lesson a priority. I couldn't wait to return the following week.

After several weeks with the beginners, I progressed to the intermediate group. I was very happy at my progress. It was excellent exercise and through regular repetition and extension of basic steps, I began to remember the combinations more easily. I drew on my knowledge of rhythm, so that even if I couldn't follow the music, I could feel the beat.

I also noticed that after a few weeks, depending on where I was in the auditorium, I was improving in my interpretation of the sound from the speakers. The music didn't seem so loud, and my brain adjusted as it had done with choir rehearsals and other loud noises.

I also used the progressive transfer from one partner to another to regularly practise speaking spontaneously. I deliberately engaged in banter with a partner or concentrated on responding to light-hearted conversation as we danced. Then I moved on to the next partner, speaking clearly and concentrating on avoiding stumbles. In this dynamic and relaxed environment where there was no pressure, it was easy to work on two types of therapy—stroke recovery and physical fitness. Physically, I felt stronger and more flexible in my mobility. I noticed that after several weeks I could confidently complete the balancing exercises that had led me to dancing.

I met many new people of different ages and backgrounds at dancVibe. Through small talk during breaks it was obvious that the common factor was each person's interest in improving dance skills—whether for exercise, health and well-being, social interaction, wedding dance practice or just for fun. For me, it achieved all of these (except the wedding dance).

I attended the dance class for more than a year. Unfortunately the club was then sold and the auditorium closed. The dance group moved to a new venue that was less convenient for me to attend. So I reluctantly looked for something else to replace modern jive, with other sustainable exercise that also had a healthy outcome—with a splash of relaxation and good fun.

Now that the 'dancing bug' had surfaced, I wondered if my longstanding love of musical theatre and old dance-based movies could extend my venture on the dancing path through to tap dancing. Searching on the Internet showed that there were several local groups for older people interested in tap dancing. But I had seen some of them performing over the years in clubs and nursing homes. I wanted something more demanding.

More searching, and I discovered BeachFit Dance. I tentatively emailed Cherie, the dance teacher and personal trainer. She was young, with a sense of humour, and I was impressed at the suggestion that people 'from 8 to 80' were welcome. Her reply, welcoming and guaranteeing, "a challenge if that's what you're looking for", spurred me to take the plunge.

When I arrived, I met a group of women of various ages (though I was clearly the oldest) who were very welcoming. To my surprise there was little that resembled my early days at tap dancing as a child. This was FAST tap! Loud, strong, active, rhythmic, challenging— and so cool! What a fantastic step up to a higher level of thinking and a boost to my balance through dance!

In the church hall in which we practised at that time, the familiar problems of reverberating sound occurred with a rush. But the exposure of the loudness at modern jive had prepared me to some degree, and I was less affected by the sound. I reverted to using the other tools such as watching and learning from what I saw, knowing that at some time, my brain would catch up in interpreting the sound. I dared to hope that it was slowly learning to cope with loud sounds.

Tap dancing was more intricate than modern jive. It was a big leap forward in terms of remembering longer sequences of dance steps to learn and perform for an upcoming concert. I had to get the rhythm right through intricate and fast-moving steps, linking the sequences in the dance. There was no room to lose concentration.

We learned several steps at each class gradually building them into a polished routine. I quickly learned that fast-paced tap is all about rhythm and precision. This suited me perfectly. I watched Cherie's demonstration of each step, practised the rhythm, watched more experienced dancers, talked it through for myself, then practised it through my feet (trying not to watch the other dancers too much). It was great therapy for dealing with the auditory processing disorder and exercising my brain!

I felt comfortable with Cherie's teaching style. Her emphasis was on fitness, learning and fun. As she had promised, she adapted her teaching to suit the ability of each dancer and guided us to proceed at our own pace. She had an innate way of making each dancer feel valued and inspired, no matter their level of skills. For those of us who struggled with more complex steps, she gave us ways of gradually working our way into success. This eased my brain into accommodating another unfamiliar task. Like the choirs and danceVibe, the BeachFit philosophy emphasised enjoyment rather than expertise. This made it easier to improve everything.

Cherie allowed me to video the dances at rehearsal, so at home I studied the video to look for repeated sections, similarities and differences in sequences. I was feeling much more confident with my analytical skills. I applied the strategy I had used for learning the sequences of sections in long pieces of classical music, and set up a plan of written notes for the tap routines. Then I practised the sections as part of my WBAs, before slowly linking each section for the whole dance. This was an excellent drill exercise done in an enjoyable way. The more I practised, the more confident I became that I would remember the dance sequences at the concert in front of an audience.

To create the clean sound of 'a cappella' tap as a group meant performing the intricate steps and long sequences exactly in time with without music. I became much more aware of how the steps created the rhythm, which in turn, helped me to improve my balance and posture.

At home I loved wearing my tap shoes, and my beautiful sportswear, and dancing my way along the hallway to the kitchen several times each day for a cup of tea. I practised my sequences and my rhythm, now through my brain and my feet! I was feeling good!

At the concert, I knew that the apprehension I felt before we performed arose from the ultimate test as to whether my strategic training approach had been successful. *Can I cope with the excitement and remember the dance?* Perhaps it was the need to be very alert when performing, but during the performance my brain could hear our combined sound with clarity. I felt excited being part of this group of women on stage. Our performance was great fun and we received excellent feedback from our audience.

A few months later, Cherie moved her business to new and larger premises. The dance studio was now adjoining a gym, run by Steve, the Gym Manager and Personal Trainer. In addition to a fantastic new dance floor, Cherie also installed equipment for pole fitness classes. This looked interesting!

I didn't know that pole 'fitness' and pole 'dancing' were poles apart. Looking at this way of improving fitness on YouTube, I wondered if it was feasible for older women, especially one looking for adventure! Cherie assured me that it was achievable, good fun, and great for building physical strength and self-confidence.

A week later, I attended my first pole fitness class. To see Cherie demonstrate some of the moves was very inspiring. She floated onto the pole with extraordinary control as if to defy gravity, twisted and turned, hung upside down by her feet and landed with the grace of a ballerina. I laughed at the prospect of me doing the same! She assured me that it was about strength and that my daily exercise program would be of great help. It involved learning about core strength, flexibility and technique.

We began with a comprehensive warm-up. I was determined and did my best to keep up with the younger women in the class. Cherie demonstrated the mechanics of how to climb the pole and gave us some exercises as preparation. It looked easy enough—but at my first few attempts, I couldn't lift both feet off the floor simultaneously. Reality check. I was a long way from moving anywhere, let alone climbing on the pole. I knew I was in for some real learning and one of the greatest physical challenges of my many adventures so far. *Can a person of my age really do this?*

Although it seemed unlikely to me that I could ever do pole, in that first class Cherie taught us some simple but beautiful moves that enabled us to gain some confidence in working with this apparatus—with my feet firmly planted on the floor. By the end of the class, I was suddenly aware of many muscles that had been dormant for years. I wasn't under any illusion about this latest challenge on which I had embarked!

At home, I returned to YouTube to look again at how this form of fitness worked. I found the Pole Dictionary that showed the mechanics of pole fitness. I spent a long time going over some of the beginners' moves to understand how it was done. I also found some examples of older women in demonstrations and competitions overseas (not in gentlemen's clubs, or with g-strings or high heels). I found a quirky example: poles installed in the swimming pool of an exclusive residential estate, thoroughly enjoyed by elderly residents on a regular basis. I was very enthusiastic about adding pole to my growing list of activities to keep me interested and challenged in exercise, beyond conventional age expectations. I couldn't wait for the next class.

Over the next few weeks I began to feel stronger and more confident when working on the pole. By five weeks I could climb and spin. Within 10 weeks I was learning a beautiful routine. Under Cherie's guidance there were other bonuses. Her positive attitude and unwavering faith in my ability to achieve success at pole, played a major role in rebuilding my self-belief. She taught me how to link mind and body, and keep reaching for the heights—literally. I liked her creative thinking, teaching me to think differently, if I encountered a difficult move. Invariably, the technique could be learned bit-by-bit from preparation and practice through to performance. The feeling of increasing muscular strength was very stimulating and empowering for my sense of well-being. The more I extended the range of pole moves over the weeks and months, the more I felt energised, physically strong and mentally confident.

Along the way, I also found that I could more easily perform aerial and inverted pole moves. These involved working more intensively and at a higher level on the pole. My brain was still waking up joints and muscles that had rarely been used. I felt stronger, healthier and more aware of each one, and how they worked together to keep me flexible and safe.

After several months, Cherie planned and organised a pole concert to showcase her students. I listened to the music for my routine in every available moment when driving, in the garden, during my WBAs and while shopping to teach my brain to section the music and visualise each segment in my choreographed routine. Ten days before the performance, I could more confidently link the sections in my mind, and had the routine firmly planted in my memory.

A week before the concert, Cherie videoed my dress rehearsal so I could look at where I could tweak and polish my performance. It was hard to believe that I was dressed in a sparkling costume of black spangled tights and top, and a matching hat. But this time there were no negative thoughts of body image. I could suddenly see results of my hard work and perseverance over the past two years since the stroke.

Six months after beginning pole, I performed my first routine to an audience, to a beautiful version of Charlie Chaplin's 'Smile'. It was nerve-wracking to complete the performance, this time alone. But with the afternoon light flowing through the high studio windows, there was a beautiful ambience in the performance space. I didn't want it to end. I performed as if I was the only person on the planet (it helped by taking off my glasses). I was in the zone.

After this performance I was keen to move to the next level of pole and test my strength and flexibility with more advanced training. Cherie began upgrading my skills.

In the intermediate class, I enjoyed the chatter of the other younger women as we worked together in the class. They showed little fear while they climbed, spun and moved, as if pole was like any other activity in their day. I was highly motivated by their enthusiasm and skills. I watched Ange's grace, Char's strength and Alyssa's confidence. I wondered if I could develop the same elegance as Ciara. Laura shared her clever techniques for mastering some tricky moves that motivated me to try harder.

I could see for myself the empowerment and self-confidence among these young women that pole had ascribed. I enjoyed the never-ending ways of improving and testing my fitness and I learned to love the freedom of pole.

I valued my heightened ability to think systematically and confidently through complicated moves. When I mastered another move on my training sheet, it was highly satisfying to know that I could keep up with some of these beautiful young women that were less than half my age. The sense of camaraderie and belonging was very precious.

It was also a way of enhancing the connection between my brain and my feet that I had begun through running. While I was by now very used to walking around home barefoot, I found it a whole new sensation relying on my feet curled around the pole to stop me falling. This extended my awareness of other joints. I became aware of increasing physical strength through my knees, fingers, hands, arms and core while performing moves in a completely disoriented position—upside down! When I accomplished a layback move and performed several crunches upside down on the pole using only my abs, feet and legs, I knew I was really progressing!

Watching Cherie practising and performing advanced and extreme moves in a safe, controlled and progressive way provided me with an excellent role model. I learned to take things slowly, gradually building my strength, stamina and my fitness. When I struggled with some moves, she said, "It's in your head, Alana".

At those times, I learned to regain my focus on the task, break it down to minute steps to keep me safe, and believe in myself. Sometimes, the systematic and gradual process of mastering a new and complex move was more exciting than becoming adept! Fortunately, I found that there were thousands of new ways that I could explore this sport. There were few boundaries, even during aging.

From stroke to pole fitness

This venture showed me that the natural and inevitable process of aging doesn't have to be a time of giving into those doomsayers of our society that impose aging before its time. There are many stereotypes of aging in media advertising that lead us to accept, what can seem to be, the inevitability of dependence: from promoting a retirement village where everyone is always smiling while sipping tea, older people always triumphing over adversity in a gentle way in the plethora of 'feel good' movies, and simple or elaborate mobility vehicles that can resemble hi-tech motorbikes.

By capitalising on the aging population, there has been an avalanche of services and products for older people that has gripped our society in recent years. But there is little talk of strategies for delaying or even preventing some of the consequences of aging beyond expensive cosmetic surgery and supermarkets full of so-called 'anti-aging' products. The shallow nature of this marketing is not about building inner strength and health through aging.

For me, through pole fitness and running I found that it is possible to participate in activities that are far-removed from the stereotypes. By building inner and physical strength to cope with the changes that are an inevitable part of aging, I have achieved a high level of self-awareness. The simple tools that I used involved educating myself and questioning what I was told, considering the options carefully and focusing on what I need, rather than what I want. This has led me to be conscious of the influences and avoid giving into unconscious consumerism. Along the way I have recognised opportunities for a full and exciting life that I would have missed if I had followed the conventional path through recovery of illness through to older age.

Risk:　　　**Uncontrolled Stress**
Solution:　　**Optimise survival by integrating work with continuous change in lifestyle activities**

While the cause of my stroke, cancer and diabetes was never investigated or considered to any degree by any HPs, I learned through my own research, that stress was the underlying factor. Over the months leading up to this disastrous event almost three years earlier, I had ignored or dismissed any symptoms that could have been indicators of hypertension.

Until that time, I hadn't experienced any major illnesses. I lived in a false sense of security, assuming that my health was good. However, I had become aware that it was getting more difficult to get around due to my increasing obesity, lack of sleep and the demands of my workload. I had little time for relaxation and had taken very few holidays at any time in my work life, actively avoiding time off as 'wasteful'.

I had always loved my business and it didn't occur to me that time out was essential. The exhilaration from building a business from scratch had always fascinated me. Empowerment came from the challenge of taking responsibility and the sense of satisfaction in self-initiated decision-making that accompanied the business as it grew.

I had learned that the demands of small business were always changing. In responding to my rapidly growing client base in the year prior to the stroke, I had skewed my priorities to almost solely focusing on my workload, in order to keep up with the demand. I lost track of how to keep on top of situations that caused stress. Perhaps this arose from complacency, ignorance or denial. But in the end, it didn't matter. The reality was that I suffered three major illnesses concurrently, any of which could have led to further illness or even an early death.

Through my vast reading, I began to learn about the nature of stress. Rod's casual remark about whether I was working too hard had lit the spark to understand the insidious nature of unmanaged stress.

If I previously thought about it at all, it was that stress was transient, it meant that I was tired, didn't sleep well, and needed some nourishing food after a frustrating day at work. I had most often turned to coffee, carbs and comfort food—thereby accelerating on a dangerous path, with no safety mechanisms in place.

I knew that stress was a natural companion of managing a business, but I hadn't consciously thought about how it could get out of hand, with such devastating outcomes. Once I was on the downward spiral it was impossible to stop. But as I began to educate myself during the early months of my recovery, I learned how stress occurs in many different unrecognised ways as part of life on a day-to-day basis. The solution was to identify its triggers, head it off and manage it carefully.

I had always prided myself on my capacity to multi-task in my busy work environment. But I hadn't stopped to think about whether this was a good strategy. Like most small business managers, I just did it!

Barbara from choir had once given me an article on the hazards of multi-tasking. While I read it with interest, I didn't act on it.

The expectations, particularly on women, to multi-task in our dynamic and fast-paced society, are marketed aggressively as part of the female psyche. This is seen in pharmaceuticals heavily advertised to assist us in coping with the inevitable demands of work, family, housekeeping and many other roles. While I hadn't fallen into the medication trap in order to cope, I had fallen into this stereotype without question.

Through my journey, I now learned that the destructive pathway that underlies unplanned multitasking, often leads to an array of health problems, frequently fuelled by stress. For me, the irony during my project was that I had to multi-task to cope with learning and establishing a vast set of new behaviours, linked across all areas of my life. So I looked at how to make multi-tasking less stressful, but more functional.

Throughout the project I had compiled and refined a long list of WBAs. I divided them into 'Active' and 'Passive' with some extra passive WBAs set up to occur while I slept. I planned each day to include several breaks consisting of only one Active WBA at any time, coupled with one or more Passive WBAs. I could concentrate on my work for the majority of my day, knowing that the other tasks required to keep me refreshed between work sessions were completed in a timely and functional manner.

This turned multi-tasking into a mostly enjoyable, organised flow of tasks with plenty of variety and choices. I became expert at functional WBAs on routine workdays and random WBAs at weekends. I continually changed my WBAs and found that boring tasks were completed quickly and efficiently. I found that I rarely felt stiff after sitting at the computer and could move around with ease.

After starting off with lists to remind me of WBAs I needed to do each day, I found that I could spontaneously engage in a useful WBA combo and effortlessly resume work after a few minutes without a list. Remaining active and alert for 10-12 hours each workday, with well-organised WBA combos, ensured time for my morning exercise and time to relax before going to bed. This also meant that I slept more restfully than I had in many years.

Examples of WBAs

Daytime Active WBAs (Vigorous *2 – 60 minutes*)	Daytime Passive WBAs (*Limited 2 – 10 minutes*)	Overnight Passive WBAs (No activity up to 14 hours)
• Sweeping (Internal/ external) • Vacuuming • Cleaning glass doors/ furniture • Cleaning kitchen benches, shelves and cupboards • Gardening • Tidying the garage • Weights training • Pole practice/ stretching • Dance routine practice	• Washing dishes • Tidying/cleaning the kitchen bedroom or bathroom • Preparing whole foods: grinding herbs and seeds, chopping food. • Preparing bulk food for dehydrating or freezing • Pickling/fermenting food • Watering the sprouts/garden • Practising piano	• Fermenting yoghurt • Fermenting vegetables • Soaking grains and legumes • Proving home made bread • Draining whey from homemade cottage cheese • Dehydrating various foods •

I started to feel the benefit of better sleep by waking more relaxed and refreshed. But it took more than 18 months to re-establish a regular sleeping pattern. This meant making it a priority—as non-negotiable as my early morning exercise—to go to bed around the same time each night and wake naturally after seven or eight hours of restful, quality sleep without the jarring sound of an alarm. This also meant that I began the day calmly with more focus and time to think about what needed to be done. By keeping my daily timetable flexible, I felt comfortable in the pace of most days. My project data shows continuous, well-controlled blood pressure and blood sugar maintained in the normal range after a rocky start.

Risk: **Returning to old habits**
Solution: **Maintain the education and momentum to do what is required to achieve and continually improve my health. Take on the challenges without fear.**

Having lost almost half of my original weight, managing risk to sustain this loss took on a new and deeper dimension from that identified in the early stage of my project. By the time two years had passed, I had made so many changes to my life, there was a risk that I would be unable to maintain the effort to sustain them for life, particularly as I aged.

There was a wealth of research that highlighted how many people reverted to old habits after losing weight, often with worse consequences than before the loss. But I saw my changing life as taking a ticket to freedom from the fog of ignorance, complacency, procrastination and poor health, through a turnstile leading to a better life. It was essential that I maintain the momentum and it was my responsibility alone, to ensure that I succeeded. Underpinning my achievements was the importance of continually educating myself every step of the way, to regain independent decision-making and control of my life.

As I waded through mountains of information on leading a positive and healthy life, I talked to many people who had experienced significant illnesses and/or low motivation. I became aware that 'being bothered' was a key to ongoing success.

Some people have been forthright in stating that they "can't be bothered" taking the steps that I found were essential to facilitate my changing lifestyle. Perhaps this is an excuse for not trying or not knowing where to start, or being confused by vague information, and unachievable, poorly defined goals suggested by some by HPs. Perhaps this is the result of living in a world of convenience with a service available for everything: accessible and affordable for most people. In general, we have learned to succumb, without question, to the 'experts' who tell us what we should do, eat, buy, wear, think and behave in all areas of our lives. Consequently, we lose our skills and give up our right to choose, then miss out on the joy and empowerment of making independent decisions. The service, often at extraordinary cost, frequently becomes the norm, sometimes to our detriment.

While overcoming a major hurdle in changing my lifestyle I have experienced the empowerment of educating myself and confidently questioning what other people suggest is best for me. Along the way, I have learned how to live a simple life, rich in friendships, with limitless cost-effective and affordable choices. I have easily found resources all around me on the fringe of a fast-paced and highly-structured society driven by powerful and persuasive marketing.

As I focused on changing my life so dramatically, I realised that the physical environment in which these changes had taken place also had to change for lifelong sustainability. I could now see things from a new perspective, to treasure what I had achieved and continue to build my strength to deal with further hurdles that may arise. In accordance with project management principles, I wanted to ensure that my new life could be managed and maintained.

At a practical level, this included modernising my kitchen as a critical part of my new lifestyle maintenance. I spoke to Danny the

Plumber, a long-time friend and excellent tradesman, to find the right builder. He spoke to Shane the Builder, who spoke to Brad the Electrician, Terry the Painter and Darren and Peter the Tilers. So I began again, with a new team, on a very different project that tested my creativity, resilience, planning, analytical skills, flexibility, negotiation skills and capacity to cope with stress. This was tested especially at one stage when my house was completely packed onto the back deck and my entire business piled in one small corner!

I drew on Shane's expertise to be the Manager for this project. I happily took on the role of the Project Manager's Manager. I had a largely ceremonial role of walking around admiring the way all team members worked. I acknowledged their attention to detail, care and pride they took in their respective jobs. They collaborated with me in what started with a kitchen, and finished with a complete refurbishment of my home. As each room in my old and neglected home revealed itself to be in need of a makeover, the team systematically worked with my (often) unconventional ideas.

I was fascinated and appreciative of their effort and meticulous detail in making things work. Shane was always calm, patient and very tactful in pointing out why some things I suggested would not work in an old home. He listened to my ideas, negotiated some modifications where necessary, and gave me time to research, analyse and think through the options, before making my decisions.

Many times over these months, I felt reassured that this project was in good hands. For me, it was less demanding than managing a whole lifestyle change, but involved learning a whole new skill set to design a home for a new lifestyle, for my senior years. It was enjoyable, creative and satisfying, supported by an expert and knowledgeable team.

I was delighted when Jordie the Apprentice gave me a simple solution to reduce the reverberation in a large room where it had sometimes been difficult to understand conversations. Brad and his offsider, Ben, worked very hard to make sure my new lighting was functional to suit my home and my business. Along the way, Brad relocated the business telephone from one room to another. This immediately fixed one aspect of my auditory processing difficulty that had plagued me for two and a half years.

Shane and his team patiently answered all of my many questions, about what they did and why they did it. We worked well together because they involved me in each decision. We collaborated and negotiated options, seeing how my ideas could be integrated into the existing structure and the planned changes for a functional, efficient and easily managed home that would suit me for many years to come. Their preferences weren't always mine, but I felt pleased with myself that I could now confidently analyse the information to make the right decision. While they respected my ideas, I acquiesced when they were clearly more knowledgeable, practical and logical.

We had many lively discussions about the challenges of renovating and the merits of healthy food and exercise. They could see the very pleasing results of their work in operation as we conducted final testing and commissioning of the kitchen with some of my gourmet lunches, before the final handover.

I worked collaboratively with Carmel, an innovative Interior Designer with exquisite taste and creativity in design. She helped me in selecting beautiful furnishings that turned rooms into stylish and comfortable living areas, blending and transforming old designs into modern spaces. I valued her effort in educating and helping me to select furnishings that suited me, and gently guiding me through decision-making. She also taught me the gentle art of doona-puffing to optimise its lightness and warmth for a good night's sleep.

Kyleigh, the Creative Gardener, used her magic to refurbish my flower garden so I could enjoy the views from my windows. I appreciated her gentle manner and the care she took with the creatures in the garden, working to keep it as free as possible of chemicals, to complement home-grown produce for my gourmet pantry. We were excited the day she found a gorgeous, tiny green frog—this was a sign of a healthy environment. She carefully integrated the flowers with the vegetable and fruit (my strawberry bed was happily crowned by a lavender bush) so I could enjoy everything in the garden and view it as functional, practical, useful and beautiful.

Initially, it was confronting to discard many of the symbols and habits of my previous life. To redesign what had been a comfort zone and embrace a totally new approach to building a new life was at once exciting, fearful, stimulating and challenging. This 'project within a project' was a test of my ability to transfer learning across environments and find proof of my skills returning through the levels of Bloom's Taxonomy.

I was excited that at last I had finally regained my capacity for creativity—the pinnacle of the Taxonomy—that had drawn all of the fragments together, particularly as it had started with such fractured beginnings. In this new project, I saw how each intricate element was inextricably linked with another, to complete the project. It was a snapshot of a project that I had started almost three years earlier, to achieve a changing lifestyle that was so important to regain my health, self-esteem and independence.

Over several months the team turned an old house into a beautiful, light, airy, and functional home that perfectly complemented my new lifestyle. They were engineers.

Chapter Twelve

Project Report: Reflections

The journey described by Adele had taken many different routes. But the journey that began at a careful and measured pace often accelerated into a fast ride as I took many side roads and adventures. I took along with me those people who wanted to share the ride and who supported me in whatever direction we took, while leaving pessimists and cynics in my wake.

My adventure to a new life started with tentative footsteps, inhibited by fear of the unknown and an unwanted lack of self-confidence. They were like the small ripples that began at the river's source, gathering volume through twists and turns to the waterfall with the power to change everything in its path, to the smooth water of the sea. I've often laughed with friends—'from stroke to pole'. And what a tumultuous journey it has been!

During these experiences I learned a great deal about my resilience. This life skill that I knew so well, re-emerged even at my lowest ebb when I knew that I was fighting for survival with three major illnesses. I had survived many challenges throughout my earlier life, as everyone does. But for me, the pinnacle was recovering from serious illness through major lifestyle change, to lead a happy, healthy and productive older life at a much higher level than expected.

As a young person, I was fortunate to have mentors where I learned valuable skills that have stayed with me for life. They provided tools for the project: Betty, an educational mentor, who many years ago taught me about lateral-thinking, 'that there is always an alternative'. I clung to this axiom throughout my educational work, my business practices, and in more recent times in changing my life. There was also Colleen, my swimming instructor, who taught me to swim at the age of 55. This fulfilled a lifelong desire, previously held back by fear resulting from a childhood near-drowning incident. I placed my trust in her to keep me safe. Her gentle encouragement and infinite patience yielded results that I had only ever imagined. The presentation of my first swimming certificate by Colleen and the staff at my local Swim Centre meant more to me that any academic award received in my professional life. It took dogged effort and perseverance even when at times I felt like it could not be achieved.

In overcoming the more recent challenges to my health, I searched for as long as I had to, in order to find answers or alternatives, believing that they were there—somewhere. This was the case when I looked vainly across Australia to find help for my auditory processing disorder. As with many solutions I eventually found it in overseas research. With a positive approach, I found strategies that were functional and led to the outcomes I desired.

When I became frustrated because I couldn't find a template for changing my lifestyle, my search resulted in my recognition that there is no template. For some individuals, the one-size-fits-all approach can be misleading, and doomed to fail.

Heather, Annette, Adele and Ken, my multidisciplined project team, never waivered in their encouragement. They supported me in making my own choices and in setting my own direction. They remained loyal, offering input into my ideas and supporting my judgment in solving problems. This generated my trust in their guidance, which undoubtedly stimulated me to greater success. From some failures came new ideas and I celebrated the small and large steps that I took in testing the limits of the ride.

The outcomes and joy of my new lifestyle has been manifested on one hand where I can choose to do whatever I want to do and be; on the other hand, I have been grateful for the guidance of people I trust. Being willing to take another step forward has involved considering their wisdom carefully, before venturing around the next bend in the road.

The lessons that I have learned have been strengthened by my capacity to succeed through determination, problem-solving, analytical skills and creativity. I have tested conventional wisdom and expectations and clung vigorously to the right to question what we are told by others, even with the risk of retribution. The right to personal choice is fundamental in preserving dignity and integrity, and in moulding a life that suits the individual, without disrespecting others.

As I walk around in our busy society today I see few people who have obviously suffered stroke. This doesn't mean that every stroke victim has noticeable outcomes such as paralysis, but in a frantic world where taking the time to speak slowly to a person with difficulty in communication is an irritation, or where a person is embarrassed because they suffer an unresolved auditory processing disorder, it is easy to become isolated, reclusive and withdrawn from society. I have often wondered how many people with outcomes of stroke, similar to me, have lost the will and the motivation to try to improve their quality of life. Perhaps they will never have the joy of being part of life again, in the way they would choose.

During the time that it took me to regain my self-belief after stroke to interact confidently and independently with others, I was reminded many times of how the loss of these freedoms was debilitating and depressing. I encountered a constant barrage of cues from some HPs, influential people, and marketing experts that coerce, frighten, bully, influence and push us to make decisions that may not always be in our best interests. The real achievement is to retain the courage to resist the need to comply with stereotypical images. It takes courage to make our own decisions and take responsibility for the outcome. The easier, but less fruitful way out, is to blame someone else when things fail.

Initially, when faced with the obstacles of three major illnesses, it was the remnants of my lateral thinking and creativity that I grasped, albeit struggling to wade through a fog caused by an injured brain. Far from being prescriptive, the principles used by my engineering clients combined with Bloom's Taxonomy gave me branches that I could hold onto, rather than be swept away by the waterfall. They enabled me to stay upright and on track.

What sometimes clouded my capacity to use them fully was undoubtedly the fear and panic that arose from my hospitalisation—that I might be permanently disabled or unable to live my life in the way that I chose, due to uninformed decisions of some HPs. Suffering shock and fear from the seeds sown in a less-than-caring service, left a legacy manifested in lack of self-confidence. This persisted for a long time and was at least as traumatic as the stroke itself, compounding and hindering my recovery, and at times appearing as an insurmountable barrier. My personal experience has taught me that self-belief is the essence of recovery.

Using principles from project management that I could constantly apply, put me in control of my world, rather than depending on others. This fundamental strategy underpinned much of the optimistic approaches to stroke recovery that I found in overseas research, and when I 'hit the wall' along my journey.

Referring to these structured principles every day, and sometimes multiple times, kept me focused with my injured brain. It was reassuring to use proven principles to provide a functional strategy to achieve success. This was in contrast to the plan mentioned in my medical file but never explained to me, or to those around me. *Did it ever exist?* When trying to wade through the myriad of services imposed on me with three serious illnesses, I knew it was up to me to forge a clear and integrated pathway with a positive focus.

My determination to continually test the limits was the catalyst for me to feel the joy of success across the various challenges that I encountered. I took up the options that felt good for me, and ran headlong with them. I learned new ways to cope with the turbulent waters. I always focused my thoughts positively on finding alternatives, to achieve outcomes that were far higher than I could ever have imagined or planned.

Were strategies such as project management principles, Bloom's Taxonomy, self-education, music and questioning conventional wisdom—useful? The answer was in recovering my language in far less than a predicted time, achieving weight loss of 45kg in 45 weeks, reversing diabetes in seven weeks, recovering from cancer surgery, remedying an auditory processing disorder and changing every aspect of my life while running a business—and writing this book. This is proof of the value of thinking laterally and drawing on even simple resources in a functional way. As unconventional and unscientific as this approach may have been, it led to outcomes that I could never have hoped for at the beginning of the journey.

That is not to say that my strategy is a panacea for anyone but me. Nor is my experience a prescription for anyone else—because everyone is different. I have never waivered from or lost track of that thought. But what my experience highlights is the value of thinking creatively. This is the seed for change and could have been lost to me as an individual, had I not questioned the value and relevance of one-size-fits-all services.

For those HPs who may dismiss my strategies as anomalous, even wacky, let them pause and think about the use of their own creativity in meeting the individual needs of patients with serious illnesses in changing their lifestyles—even when working within the umbrella of complex services and evidence-based practice.

Stifling or disregarding creativity is to risk wasting resources and achieving less than optimal outcomes when delegated with someone else's care. It shows little empathy, knowledge or understanding of how that person's life experiences influence their recovery. In some cases, the 'care' has been lost from some healthcare services.

At no time during my project did I subscribe to the elusive concept of 'reaching my potential', especially by 12 months after the stroke. I had always seen this concept as indefinable and therefore unattainable. With an injured brain, and the urgency to remediate the damage as quickly as possible, I could never have found a pathway to success through the maze of colloquialisms, motivational quotes, vagaries and directives that always accompany discussion of human potential.

In my lifetime thus far, I have never met or read about anyone who has ever proven that they have reached it. If I do, I will ask them, "So, what's next?"

Setting a goal to reach our potential can be restrictive in itself. Each day I learn something new that beckons with a challenge to do more. I have learned to maximise every day, every moment, in every aspect of my life, for life.

On reflection, it's too easy to give in to the aging process through images that constantly bombard and confront us in our society. The reality is far from these images. From some of my clients I have learned that in the language of aggressive sales industry advertising, targeting seniors (or anyone else) is called 'grooming the consumer.' There is irony even for those people who can afford the advertised luxuries, 'must haves' and stereotypical lifestyle of 'free-of-care' retirees.

In succumbing to the illusion, we risk giving away choice, opportunities and active participation in decision-making. In the broader context, such as when accessing health services, losing these functions leads to the inevitable pathway of dependence, loss of integrity and forfeited individuality. My brush with this world as a stroke patient was frightening.

I am a member of the Baby Boomer Army—the generation that inherited all the tools to do the job—and we have practised our skills throughout our lives to achieve our level of expertise. We are confident, educated, literate, articulate and tech-savvy. We are analytical, creative and compassionate. We question what others impose on us because we know that the right to choose is too precious to lose. We are the instigators of change. But if we allow ourselves to drift into the waterfall, we sometimes need the universe to kick us back into our destiny.

Email to Adele:
Out of the Fog is finished. But the journey is still going…. and the best is yet to come!

Thanks

From the moment of suffering a devastating stroke, I benefitted from the support and resources of people that I trusted, and who showed unfailing belief in my capacity to regain my skills and rebuild my life. For all of them, those I have mentioned and those I may have inadvertently left out, I have unlimited gratitude.

To my dear friend Heather, who has stood by me over the years from the first steps in setting up my business, through to supporting me unconditionally during the challenges of this more recent project, how can I thank you enough? I owe lifelong appreciation for your friendship and good counsel.

To Annette, thanks for your persistence, lateral-thinking and warm friendship during days of self-doubt, but importantly for restoring my precious bond with music. To William, thank you for being my 'ears' when my brain couldn't hear.

To Adele, thank you for your gentle inspiration, and showing me that there are still some health professionals that are prepared to push the limits. You are a sad loss to health services, but I am richer for having shared my journey with you and the universe.

Thanks to Frank, my wonderful business manager, for your meticulous attention to detail, and keeping everything running correctly (including my words), when my brain was tired. Thanks to Lorraine, always organised and practical, for stepping in to streamline my business procedures when my brain felt scrambled and afraid. Thanks to Greg, my accountant and his staff, Anne and Michaela, who were always there to sort out the business problems when my brain refused to work.

To Bernard, my IT Consultant, thanks for always having the solutions and calming my anxiety when technical problems occurred, and to Elizabeth, whose longstanding friendship I have always enjoyed.

Cherie, you never cease to amaze me with your strength and creativity. Thank you for motivating me to test the physical and psychological boundaries beyond our images of aging. You taught me to trust my brain and my body again!

John and Winsome, thanks for your friendship, always available and positive. Pam, thank you for having the coffee ready on many occasions when I needed a chat. Thanks to Barbara and Ralph, whose jovial company provided much-needed respite in a busy life. One day, I'll take that holiday to see the leaning palm trees!

To Val and Nance, my car therapists. Thank you for your friendship and humour, shared at many lively evenings and car trips. Thanks to Nina who was only ever a phone call away. Lynda, thank you for your advocacy and belief in justice for vulnerable people.

I have been so lucky with Ken, my wonderful GP, who supported me when I ventured beyond conventional medical approaches, and kept me motivated with gold stars for my successes. Thank you to David, my Oncology Surgeon, André, my Medical Oncologist and your wonderful teams in breast cancer services whose professionalism and honesty gave me hope and strength in overcoming the fear of cancer.

Barb didn't live to see *Out of the Fog* published, but she was with me along the way. I will always treasure her simple kindness and her big heart.

For the divas and divos of the choirs whose love and friendship was my inspiration—you will always be in my thoughts. Thank you so much for believing in me and taking my faltering steps to recovery in your stride. Your music, friendship and support are immeasurable and inspirational. Love is always in the air.

Thanks to Jackie and Kevin, my long-time friends, who have waited for many years for me to produce a book. I finally did it!

About the Author

Alana Henderson has worked for many years as an adult educator, public speaker, and editor. She lives in New South Wales, Australia.

Printed in the United States
By Bookmasters